T0288327

'an extraordinarily good piece of writing'
—Kim Hill (Radio New Zealand)

'a deeply personal, delightfully told memoir of a father, who happened to be New Zealand's "most gifted and significant literary editor of his generation". It's powerfully honest, full of love and pain'
—Sonja de Friez, Nine to Noon (Radio New Zealand)

'I trust a memoirist who is as hard on himself as on everyone else'
—Stephen Stratford, *New Zealand Listener*

'Robin Dudding's son Adam has written a brave, unsparing, affectionate, critical and impartial book in this voyage around his father. It does justice to Robin's struggles and achievements as well as to the havoc he wrought'
—Paul Little, *North and South*

'an extraordinarily candid, sad, funny, exhilarating and chastening story, written with a sharp eye for telling detail, a tolerant sense of humour and a clear prose style that makes it a pleasure to read'
—Nicholas Reid, *Sunday Star-Times*

My Father's Island

A Memoir

Adam Dudding

Victoria University Press

TE WHARE WĀNANGA O TE ŪPOKO O TE IKA A MĀUI
VICTORIA
UNIVERSITY OF WELLINGTON

VICTORIA UNIVERSITY PRESS
Victoria University of Wellington
PO Box 600 Wellington
vup.victoria.ac.nz

First published 2016

National Library of New Zealand Cataloguing-in-Publication Data

Dudding, Adam.
My father's island : a memoir / Adam Dudding.
ISBN 978-1-77656-082-0
1. Dudding, Robin. 2. Periodical editors—New Zealand—Biography.
I. Title.
070.51092—DC 23

Printed in China by 1010 Printing International

To my family

Contents

I. Funeral

My FATHER'S FACE was always thin, even before his years of ill health, but no one has told the mortician that. He has restored Dad to a Platonic ideal of the ageing, bearded patriarch – plumped out the deep cheek hollows, smoothed his frown-lined forehead, painted over the broken blood vessels on his nose, deflated the bags that used to hammock beneath his eyes.

His skin is a healthy pinkish colour, not the grey I've grown used to, and his white beard has been brushed up to double its normal thickness. I haven't seen it so voluminous and dense since the 1970s, when it was still black and extended halfway down his chest and almost as far width-wise. His lips are closed, but only just, as if he's thought of something quite funny and is considering whether to say it out loud.

The coffin is balanced on a folding trestle in the bedroom I used to share with my youngest sister. We've walked the coffin down the garden path – an uncle, two sisters, a couple of my nephews and me – past the sandpit built for grandkids and neighbourhood children but now colonised by Dad's staked tomatoes, across the treacherously rotten wooden deck and through the French door which, three decades after installation, can still only be secured by wedging a thrice-folded piece of paper between jamb and door.

Younger nieces and nephews look on. One asks why, if this is a cardboard eco-coffin, it looks just like wood. Another ducks under the coffin to assure himself the undertaker has set up the trestle correctly.

My father lies there for a day and a half, never quite getting round to telling his joke. I don't remember doing it, but I imagine that I touch his cheek and that it is cold and waxy. Apart from the closed eyes, he reminds me of the heroic portrait of Karl Marx on one of the USSR stamps someone gave me for my album when I was eight. Dad looks healthier dead than he has for some years.

A month earlier we'd gone for a meal at a Korean restaurant with Formica tables and strip lighting to mark his and Mum's 50th wedding anniversary.

By then, Dad had his oxygen tank with him all the time, the plastic tubing hooked around ears and nose like an ill-fitting military chinstrap. He kept resting his head on his hand and taking anxious little sipping breaths. He barely ate or spoke.

Chewing and swallowing were becoming too difficult, the latest in a grim checklist of the activities systematically ruled out by emphysema over a decade and a half. First, the running and cycling and strenuous gardening. Later, lifting grandchildren and walking long distances. Later still, walking even short distances. Then driving. Then reading out loud to grandchildren. And then, near the end, swimming (he had clung to that for so long), walking across a room without stopping for rests, and sitting up straight in a chair without feeling like shit.

I took photos that day, annoying everyone by shoving a digital camera in their face for individual close-ups.

We were getting used to Dad's semi-absent status at occasions like this, so it didn't seem too callous that we were still trying to enjoy ourselves even if one of the two guests of honour was plainly having a bad time.

I'm looking at the photos now. An adult nephew gurns. A brother-in-law looks startled; his daughter grins. Another nephew blows across the top of his soft-drink bottle and his brother is chewing his chopsticks. Another brother-in-law has puffed his cheeks out and crossed his eyes. In her photo my mother has pursed her lips in what I think is amusement, and she's looking ceiling-ward.

The photo of Dad, which I think is the last I took of him alive, is awful. He stares down the barrel of the camera, too exhausted even to pull a silly face or an ironic grin. He's thin and grey. His eyes, though, are as piercing as ever. He knows the game is almost up.

A couple of weeks after that meal, Dad dictated an email (my sister Anna typed) to his six children, thanking us for the new bed we'd bought as their anniversary gift.

'It's absolutely lovely to lie on,' he wrote. 'No movement at all and I don't think either of us will fall out of this one [. . .] Many, many thanks and lots of love.'

The bed we'd replaced wasn't entirely unusable – just old and broken down and squishy and, as the email suggested, prone to ejecting sleepers – but once upon a time my parents' bed had been one of the two mortal embarrassments that made me reluctant to bring friends home from school.

From the time I was three, our family of eight lived in a two-bedroom house in Torbay, the second-to-last major bay of Auckland's North Shore as you head north. Even with children stacked into a triple bunk (the topmost the perfect height for graffitiing the ceiling) and a trundle bed, there weren't enough bedrooms for Mum and Dad, so their double bed was in the corner of the living room (or in the back garden, where on cloudless summer nights they'd drag the mattress and bedding, creating a brief mystery in the morning for children looking for a bed to climb into).

Once old enough to compare our home with other families', I realised this was unconventional and thus terrible. If a school friend visited, I'd claim the bed was actually a really big, flat couch, then suggest we stop talking about it and go play in the bamboo forest at the end of our section. Older still, I came to admire the eccentricity of the public bed, which was just as well, as even after the house gained two extra bedrooms and four children left home the double bed stayed in the living room for years.

The bed was nothing, though, compared with our toilet.

For the first half of last century, much of the Shore had no sewers, so toilets were semi-detached affairs whose small tanks of shit and piss were collected by the 'night soil man'. When sewers were installed in the mid-1960s, most people put their new loo somewhere inside. Dad didn't.

To find our toilet, you had to go out the back door of the house and down some wooden stairs that were generally slick with algae, missing several steps, or both. (After the stairs rotted completely, Dad replaced them with a sloping plank, with smaller boards nailed width-wise to reduce the chance of skating to the bottom.)

Once at the bottom of the stairs you entered the wash-house – a narrow, tunnel-like lean-to butted against the broken fibrolite exterior of the house, with its own broken louvre windows and cracked concrete floor. Through the holes in the wall you could catch glimpses of the dark, spider-filled crawlspace under the house. Along the other wall was a noisy, rust-coated chest freezer, whose interior was melted and smoke-blackened from the explosion that followed when Dad put a kerosene heater inside to defrost it and closed the lid.

The toilet cubicle itself was separated from the wash-house by a small curtain. Inside, the bowl was tilted off-square, as the concrete floor there was cracked too. Depending on household finances, there would sometimes be shop-bought toilet paper, and sometimes tidily torn squares of newspaper impaled on a nail. Mum always claimed that once you'd crumpled and rubbed a piece of inky newsprint between your hands for a while it was as good as the real thing, but that was a lie. To save on water bills, Dad had put a large brick in the cistern that reduced the amount of water used per flush, and he'd also added a lead weight to the flusher mechanism so you had to hold it down for the duration, making a swift exit impossible.

By day, all this was embarrassing; by night it was terrifying. At 10, I was still asking my mother to accompany me to the loo after dark. Fortunately Dad encouraged me to wee on his citrus trees on the other side of the house, which slightly reduced the number of visits needed.

My embarrassment reached its zenith when I was 11 and brought home for the first time my new best friend, Philip. I'd already been often to his house, which had many bedrooms, a swimming pool, a games room with a pool table and dartboard, and an Atari videogame console, and couldn't put off the return visit forever.

When Philip said he needed to go to the toilet I offered a lemon tree, but he said he needed the real thing. I simply couldn't bring myself to tell him where the toilet was. Increasingly desperate, he went searching, but didn't think to look beyond the back door.

'I'm really sorry,' I said. 'We actually don't have a toilet.'

Philip grabbed his schoolbag and ran the hilly mile to his own home.

In any case, Dad got just 14 sleeps in the lovely new bed.

Around three in the morning on Monday the 21st of April 2008, he got out of bed, probably with the aim of heading for the loo – still outside, but now accessible via a sturdy new staircase, complete with handrail and rain-shelter.

He stood, then fell to the floor.

My brother-in-law Graham, lodging at my parents' house while in Auckland for a new job, heard my mother, Lois, trying to call his name. Four years earlier Mum had suffered a major stroke that affected her right side and her speech, so her words didn't always come out right.

When Graham reached their room (my parents had, eventually, laid claim to a bedroom), Dad was lying naked on the floor, unconscious or very nearly. To Graham it seemed like he was still there, but his eyes were closed and he couldn't speak. He wasn't exactly dead, but he was awfully heavy.

Graham lifted him back onto the new bed, shaking him and shouting at him to wake up. Mum was still lying on the other side. Graham told her to press the button on her medical alarm pendant. Dad wasn't breathing so Graham began mouth-to-mouth.

When the ambulance arrived the first thing they did was drag Dad back off the soft new bed onto the hard floor, the better to perform CPR. It looked like he'd had a massive heart attack. They zapped him with their defibrillator paddles, then put him on a stretcher and carried him to the ambulance.

As Graham stripped the bed and mopped the floor, the sibling phone-tree tipped us out of our beds around the country – I don't remember which sister called me. I crept from my sleeping house and began the short drive to Sealy Road, but before I got there I got another call telling me to head for the hospital.

I drove, gritty-eyed and dazed, jaw clenched with adrenaline, through the empty suburban streets. I was in a bubble, disconnected from the real world, like I was halfway through a long-haul flight, in neither one place nor another.

I was already taking it for granted that this was a heart attack, and that even if Dad was still alive he wouldn't be for long; that his heart, grown large in compensation for pumping blood that wasn't carrying enough oxygen, was in no shape to recover from anything.

The sun wasn't up yet. As I drove I made more calls – to my wife, to my sisters. Should we wake our two young children and get them to the hospital before he dies? Do I need to hand over any projects at work if I take a few days off? What about Dad's honorary doctorate ceremony on Wednesday evening – what will we do about that?

Not far from the hospital, as I passed the row of pines lining the Pupuke golf course, I stopped thinking and cried for a bit.

At the hospital Dad was in his own room, on his back on a wheeled bed, eyes closed, a blood-oxygen sensor clipped to one of his grey fingers like a giant clothes-peg. Mum and two of my sisters, Anna and Rachel, were already there.

The monitor by his side showed his impossibly fast pulse and unfeasibly low blood-oxygen levels. Dad's heart had been restarted but the rhythms were all wrong. He is more or less brain-dead, said the doctor. There is nothing they can do. Do we want to have the monitors and wires removed?

We do.

I'm not sure how long we sat there with him – perhaps an hour. At some point, another sister, Melissa, arrived. We held Dad's large, heavy hands. We talked to him, and sang a quiet version of the Harry Belafonte calypso 'Yellow Bird'.

After a time, Dad's big bony chest – the secret behind his extraordinary ability to float on his back with arms folded lazily behind his head, as if he were in the Dead Sea rather than the Hauraki Gulf – seemed to be still, but every 20 seconds or so it heaved up, then down, accompanied by a long rasping wheeze.

We sat, and talked to him, and watched. The gaps between breaths lengthened, then his chest rose and fell and stayed there.

Mum was sitting by his shoulder. She gave a sob that was more like a roar, and bent down till her face touched his.

At 7am the wider family was gathering. They'd moved Dad to a tiny side room, and we crowded around the bed, overflowing into the hallway, my children jiggling on the knees of their much older cousins and weighing up the invitation to touch their dead grandfather if they wanted. The adults had other decisions to make – about undertakers and the funeral and where the body would go next.

The doctor needed to ask us about something else, too.

It was early Monday morning, and Dad had spent six hours on Sunday at the same hospital, sitting in Accident and Emergency with my sister Rachel, waiting to have a nasty wound on his leg treated. (That fucking new bed! He'd been walking around it and, unused to its generous dimensions, brushed his leg against its corner. His skin, tissue-paper-thin from age and from the steroids he took to eke out the last remnants of lung function, had torn back like the skin of an overripe plum, bloodily bunching back under itself.)

It's hospital policy, said the doctor, to investigate any death that occurs shortly after someone has been discharged, just in case doctors missed something they shouldn't have. Do we wish to lay a formal complaint?

We didn't. Who knows – perhaps the hospital's lamentably slow service had in fact been the death of him. But what's the point of blaming the final straw when you've known for a long time that the camel's back is at breaking point? And, we were all thinking, if not yet saying out loud, that a quick exit was probably preferable to what Dad had been enduring.

Still, it would have been nice if he'd been able to hang in there just a little longer. In two days he was meant to be receiving an honorary doctorate of literature from Auckland University. The English professors who'd put him up for the award said, in their nomination letter, that Dad wasn't exactly a household name, but he was New Zealand's 'most gifted and significant literary editor of his generation'.

Dad had been half-dreading the ceremony – the crowds, the physical discomfort, the fact that he'd probably have to go on stage in a wheelchair – but he was chuffed to have received such heavy-duty recognition.

The ceremony went ahead anyway, with two of my sisters collecting a certificate and handshake on Dad's behalf. Amid the congratulations and condolences I felt a bit sorry for the poet Vincent O'Sullivan, who was getting an honorary degree in the same ceremony – the evening was rather dominated by the pathos of an award that became posthumous by a whisker.

A day or two before the funeral I was in my father's study, sitting at his big cluttered desk, trying to figure out how to download some photographs from his ailing computer for a slideshow at the wake.

His old rotary-dialler telephone rang. It was a newspaper reporter.

'I'm calling from the *Dominion Post*. Do I have the right number for the family of Robin Dudding?'

As I answered I looked out the window overlooking the back garden, which slopes sharply down and then up again, split at the bottom by a stream that was once a few centimetres across but carved itself into a three-metre-wide chasm during successive winter downpours. After one big storm, a huge piece of earth caved in and washed away, creating a dark tunnel that ran several metres into the wet clay. Once the rain stopped, Dad found a couple of torches and persuaded a friend to come caving in his garden. The tunnel itself collapsed a few weeks later. A year or so after that, Dad got someone to dump a couple of tonnes of broken concrete pieces at our front gate, then made me help him lug them all down and toss them into our ever-growing canyon. He never fully explained what this was meant to achieve.

The reporter was asking me about Dad's early career. I got the feeling she'd called not so much because she had heard that a mighty totara of New Zealand literature had fallen, but rather to follow up an intriguing death notice about an old man who dropped dead days before he was meant to receive an award.

I'm a newspaper reporter. Occasionally I ring up relatives of the recently dead and ask intrusive questions. I'm always slightly amazed that people answer them, but now I understood.

I was on a high – a mixture of busyness and emotional intensity and lack of sleep. I'd been thinking and talking about little other than my father for the past 72 hours. Ten paces from where I was sitting, his body was lying in a box. I'd just been looking at photos of him spanning 70 years, making notes for a funeral speech, talking with my mother and sisters. Of course I could help the reporter out with a few details about who Dad was. She had trouble shutting me up.

I realised I was feeling proud. It was a reawakening of that almost-forgotten feeling I'd had when I was small that the books and magazines he made were somehow noble and important, even if when he parcelled up 10 copies of *Islands* in brown paper for my primary school fair they sat unsold on the book stall long after the last Len Deighton novel had gone for 5 cents.

All week, my mind kept slipping into an amnesiac loop. Focussed on some funeral task – flicking through my computer looking for the right tune to use as the slideshow backing, looking through the *Yellow Pages* for the string quartet Mum said she wanted playing at the wake – I'd totally forget my father was dead. Then, with a falling jolt,

I'd remember. Shit. That's right. He's dead. Impossible.

When my sisters and I divvied up the funeral chores I said I'd design the order of service. After all, this was the stuff Dad taught me, taught us all: typefaces, serifs, leading, gutters, margins, italics, small caps, hanging indents, ellipses, hyphens, en dashes, em dashes, semicolons and full stops, widows and orphans, the pros and cons of the Oxford comma, and the need to double-check spellings and quotations and dates.

I was returning a 37-year-old favour. A month after I was born, the first son after five daughters, my parents threw a party. Dad printed the invitation using hand-set text and illustrations from vintage metal printers' blocks. On the front was an ornate drawing of a four-poster bed, and inside another of a giant stork pulling a baby in a chariot and the words *By God, I have a son!* It was silly but beautifully made. The document marking Dad's exit should look just as good.

In my haste, I screwed up. I put his date of death as April 20 rather than 21. When I noticed it on the day of the funeral, I was briefly furious at myself, then decided to think of it a cosmic joke – live by the typo, die by the typo, something like that.*

---

* I messed up something else too. Dad's publications followed the standard practice (dying out now) of putting the first few words of each story in small caps, miniature capitals redrawn to be the height of a lowercase x. As a sort of tribute, I put his name in small caps in the order of service – ROBIN NELSON DUDDING. But I did it on my laptop using software that fakes small caps by simply scaling down ordinary capitals. This, Dad taught me, is an abomination because the line weight of each letter shrinks along with the height, leaving it looking spindly. It's the difference between THESE ELEGANT WORDS and THESE DREADFUL ONES. I didn't spot the error until years later, and luckily just about no one else could care less. All the same, sorry, Dad.

My parents' house is teeming with relatives and friends. There's not much black and the women aren't wearing hats, but several men are in suits. I'm wearing a three-piece I bought 10 years ago for a fancy occasion – the only suit I've ever owned. I seldom wear it though – it's black and has a slightly eccentric three-quarter-length jacket which I worry makes me look like an undertaker.

The actual undertaker looks uncannily like Dad: tall and thin-faced and with a large grey beard. A couple of times I spot him out of the corner of my eye and do a lurching double take. Shit. That's right. He's dead. He's lying there in the bedroom with the lid off the casket for anyone who wants a final glance.

Through the open door I see my six-year-old son, hugged to the hip of his adult cousin Joe, looking solemnly down at their grandfather, still not sure if he wants to touch him.

Dad's younger brother Ian calls for quiet so he can say a brief 'goodbye to big brother'. He recalls the time Robin crashed their father's van into a haystack, and his admiration of the way Robin stood up to their father's strictness and bullying. He remembers his mother getting a letter from Robin once he'd left home and moved to Auckland to be a journalist.

'Robin had no money. He hadn't got a job with the *Star* at that stage,' says Ian. 'He was telling Mum what it was like sleeping in the graveyard, and how he had to keep moving halfway through the night, because the rats were disturbing him. He was complaining that he'd lent a book of poetry to a fellow that he'd been discussing poetry with beside one of the gravestones, and unfortunately the chap hadn't returned his book.'

After we've loaded the coffin into the back of my brother-in-law's Ford Falcon station wagon for the trip to the cemetery, the undertaker wants a word with me.

'Where did you get your suit?'

'London,' I say. 'From that Spanish chain store, Zara. About 10 years ago.'

'Ah, that explains it,' he says. 'I can't find a suit like that anywhere in New Zealand.'

He looks me up and down again.

'That's a nice suit.'

We drive to the Schnapper Rock Road cemetery, which serves much of the North Shore and is as sprawling and charmless as the newly developed suburbs surrounding it.

A hundred or so mourners balance themselves on the slope. My oldest sister, Rachel, reads a eulogy. My wife reads a poem that my mother wrote in the late 1950s and which Dad published in his first magazine.

It's rather racy, with lines that go: 'I shall love you in the joy-filled spirit at night, / for the love of the racing muscle'. We've warned Mum it will be read, but I think she's forgotten, and she mutters a half-scandalised 'Oh really!'

We sing a few of Dad's favourite songs – 'Molly Malone' and 'Clementine' and 'Yellow Bird' – and a granddaughter reads out a poem she's written. Then the youngest of the grandchildren takes round baskets of stuff that Uncle Ian has collected from the garden – persimmon, feijoa, tamarillo, apple, ferns, flowers whose names I've never been able to remember – and we all hiff something onto the cardboard eco-coffin before we leave.

There are so many stories. In Rachel's eulogy at the grave she talks of Dad leading backyard golf games with a hockey stick, and of visiting friends being chased with false teeth.

At the wake at the Milford Cruising Club, it seems everyone has prepared a speech: me, my sisters, friends and partners and ex-boyfriends of my sisters who've been scarred or uplifted by their encounters with Dad, writers he once published or challenged to ping-pong or both, workmates from the *Listener*, old friends.

I've heard most of the family legends, so I'm more intrigued by the stories told by people I don't know well or haven't seen for decades.

Our friend Rose Beauchamp paints an idyllic picture of our family when we were living in Christchurch in the early 70s, when Rose was married to the writer Ian Wedde and had a young family.

'You might arrive and find Lois sitting in a tree, reading a book, because it was too stressful in the house, and Robin would be probably cooking something, and there would be examination of Adelle Davis's cookbooks as to what we were meant to be eating, and chickens to discuss and so on. I became aware that being a parent wasn't such a bad thing.'

Belinda, a school friend of my sister Ruth, tells how she and a friend flew up from Christchurch to visit us in Auckland soon after we'd moved back north. On their last night together the three friends slept on the fold-down bed in the back of Dad's Ford Transit. They were disturbed by some movement in the night, then nodded back off, but woke in the morning to find the van had been driven to the beach by Dad, who'd left them there with the back doors wide open to the sea view.

'Three 14-year-olds in our nighties, down on the beach with a plane to catch in two hours. We had to run home to

Sealy Road, with all these men and neighbours yelling out things as we went. I still cringe.'

Another friend, a champion storyteller named Ron, makes a shaggy-dog story out of the time he and Dad built new fowl-houses to a far higher construction standard than our falling-down home, then christened the buildings (and tested the guttering) by pouring bottles of beer on the roof.

Like everyone, Ron slips between tenses when talking about the dead man.

'Robin is such a kid. That night, we slept in the chicken coop. It was a great night – that coop was spotless. Robin was in one little cubicle, I was in another. It was a lovely moment. He was a great child.'

Other stories I know but have half forgotten. My parents' old friend Ian Free remembers the time in the early 80s when Dad arranged a street party to celebrate the completion by council workmen of Sealy Road's new footpath.

'We dressed up the old Hillman Super Minx with a couple of flagpoles,' says Ian, 'and we flew flags from the front mudguards, and we dressed up.'

I remember Ian's flamboyant arrival, with fake mayoral chains around his neck, but the two things that really stick in my mind from that day are that Dot from next door baked a cake in the shape of our street, complete with grey icing for the footpath, and that Mr Konings from across the road turned out to be an arcade videogame salesman. He lugged a huge two-player Donkey Kong machine out onto the footpath, removing the coin box so you would play forever with one recycled 20-cent coin. It felt like owning a goose that laid golden eggs.

Funerals are where nice things are said, but if you care to

hear it, there's an undercurrent of something else.

Those halcyon childhood days, says Rachel, were winding down by the time the youngest siblings came along. 'Dad had got a bit grouchy – we'll generously ascribe that to pain in his arthritic hips.'

Anna – the sister closest in age to me – is more direct.

'He was a tough dad,' she says, her voice cracking. 'He never said "yes"; it was always "maybe". Whenever you walked in the door he said, "What took you so long?"' In recent years, she confesses, 'I've been cross with him a lot.'

She tries to balance these awkward heresies by insisting she has 'so many really, really good memories' of Dad's vigour and sense of fun, but the dark note has been struck.

A school friend of my sister Melissa tells a complicated yarn whose main point is that when he was a teenager Dad mercilessly insulted him, teased him about his last name, and called him a dimwit.

Graham, the brother-in-law who gave Dad CPR, tells how after he and Ruth (who aren't married) announced she was pregnant, Dad brought out a .22 rifle and left it on the dining table, as some sort of heavy-handed joke about shotgun weddings. Graham insists it's an example of 'Robin's sense of humour and fun', but really it's a story about how he sometimes got a kick out of making people feel uncomfortable.

Near the end of the wake, a painter I don't recognise gets up and makes a long, confusing speech about how Dad was, or wasn't, like the painters Colin McCahon and Pat Hanly. The painter says: 'One of Robin's greatest achievements was that, though involved in the arts in an integral way, he would never have had to apologise to his children', and I think, 'Really? Where did you hear that?'

I always feel vaguely irritated when someone's talking about a dead person and they say such-and-such is 'what they would have wanted'. It's the kind of thing an avaricious in-law might say just before disappearing into the night with a disputed family heirloom. Or maybe I don't like the implicit religiosity, as if the dead could give a toss what we do once they're gone.

All the same, I feel that my mother and my sisters and I, and all the people who sang and spoke and read poems or just turned up, have done the old bastard proud.

Dad was a creator of minor family traditions – forcing would-be sons-in-law to play him at ping-pong for a daughter's hand in marriage; insisting that Christmas morning presents be unwrapped en masse in the parental double bed after a breakfast of scrambled eggs; the provision of a packet of chewing gum for any child sitting a school exam. So ad hoc funeral rituals, like throwing feijoas on his coffin, or having a daughter-in-law read an erotic poem written by his wife, feel right.

A few weeks later, though, Anna finds an unsigned draft of a will Dad wrote in 1994. It's a brief note essentially leaving everything to Mum, and has a familiar undertone of passive-aggressive complaint: 'As I haven't had time (or attracted much interest) in preparing aforesaid document – let me just express preferences for some other poor bugger to work out . . .'

As for his funeral wishes, all he wrote was: 'On death: burial or cremation, whatever suits. NO SERVICE of any kind, but wake at 4 Sealy Rd Torbay, with keg of Guinness provided from my estate.'

We got it wrong on just about every count, but I think we were still near enough.

2. Damascus

It's sometime in the late 1980s. My father's study smells of tobacco and unflued kerosene heater and old paper. Dad is sitting at the wide wooden desk that's all but submerged in mounds of paper, but he's scalloped out enough space for two piles of long, skinny galley proofs, face up on the right, face down to the left. He's reading aloud as fast as we can manage, droning the syllables like a horse-racing commentator.

> . . . on-this-day-comma-the-seventh-day-comma-she-also-put-away-her-husbands-poss-s-weekday-one-word-clay-pipe-and-replaced-it-with-his-sunday-cap-s-birchwood-one-word-stop . . .

I'm sitting to his left, holding copy – silently comparing what he's saying against the words in my pile of marked-up typescripts, listening for the skipped lines and missing punctuation inflicted on the text by the typesetters as they made the galleys. Pure typos aren't my responsibility – Dad is correcting them as he goes with his fine-tipped red BIC ballpoint – but if I think I spot a difference I pause the horse race: 'I've got greatgrandmother as one word, not hyphenated', or 'Did you say comma?'

When I'm holding copy my mind is often elsewhere, each sentence a string of sounds processed then discarded. This time, though, I'm listening to the words.

It's a short story, set in the 1930s or thereabouts, about the narrator's then-young great-grandmother, who wants a fur coat but whose husband refuses to buy her one. Over the next few months the great-grandmother covertly bakes and sells biscuits to passing schoolchildren and saves her pennies. Eventually, when she proudly shows her husband the coat she has bought herself, he says nothing and stalks out of the house. The next day he trades it in at the pawn shop and keeps the money. The coat is never seen again and nor is the money. Silly great-grandmother got it wrong. The End.

It's a softly spoken story with a sting in its tail, and the feminist subtext is pointed but not heavy-handed. It's a really good story.

Dad turns his page and hands me the typescript of the next short story (or poem or critical essay or review) – one of the precious things he has sifted and shuffled to create the latest issue of his literary 'quarterly', though the last time *Islands* actually appeared four times in one year was almost a decade ago. He starts to read, and I'm scanning my page, but I'm still thinking about that last story.

There's nothing odd about my father publishing overtly feminist fiction. He's progressive, liberal, open-minded, enlightened – all that. He's been championing the work of women and men, Māori and Pākehā, gay and straight, young and old, rebels and conservatives, for decades now, as long as it's *good*. And if it's *good*, why wouldn't he publish a story that cleverly and entertainingly derides patriarchal constraints on women's economic autonomy and choices in the early 20th century and, by inference, in the late 20th century?

Well, maybe because of this: it is only a matter of weeks since my father went to my mother's 'office' (actually a tiny side-table crammed into a corner of the sitting room and stacked high with books and papers), tipped the contents onto the floor and took the table out to the back garden, where he covered it with boxes of tomato seedlings. When Mum got home her things were still scattered on the floor: pens, pencils, textbooks and notes from her course in teaching English as a second language, which was her latest attempt to find a way back into the working world after three decades raising children.

His annexation of her minuscule territory is only the latest in years of attacks on her attempts to carve out something of her own. He has raged and shouted when she cut her beautiful long hair short. He has told her, this is *my* house, not *our* house. He has binned the letters that arrived for Lois Miller when she experimented with reviving her maiden name. She has no bank account of her own and no money beyond the cash he doles out for groceries.

She has continued to cook his lunch and dinner, wash his clothes, clean his house, make his bed, and when bookish visitors call she brings out plates of home-baked bread and crackers and sliced cheese and tomatoes and raisins and cups of tea, and everyone sits and talks about books and chickens and children and life and how wonderful Lois's baking is.

That's why the story about the great-grandmother stays with me. It's as if the author has been listening at our window.

I can't remember if I challenge Dad about the hypocrisy of his editorial decisions, but I probably do. I'm 15 or so, and full of the infinite wisdom and certainty of the teenager who's recently figured out that adults, especially his parents, are imperfect.

Sometimes, when he's being particularly horrid, I'll ask, 'Why are you such a prick to Mum?' He never answers of course, but then, he never answers any questions. He has a simple trick for never losing an argument, especially in a house full of people who like to have the last word: say nothing at all, and if the questions don't stop, just stand up and walk out of the room.

3. Letters

Not long after I tell my mother and sisters I've decided to write a book about Dad, my sister Melissa drops off a tea-chest-sized cardboard box full of chokingly musty papers (and, mystifyingly, three even mustier cushions).

The papers are two-thirds junk – crap collected over the decades by Dad's mother Winifred at the family home in Hastings, then passed on after her death and once again after Dad's.

Junk, but intriguing all the same: recipes and shopping lists jotted on scraps of notepaper, brown paper bags and smoothed-out sheets of used Christmas paper, cardboard cereal boxes cut into pieces to reuse as jotting paper, unsent sympathy cards, parish newsletters, a handwritten list of Latin names for trees, a brochure for the European tour she and Grandad took in 1967, award certificates for Grandad's prizewinning fowls, an exercise book full of handwritten tips for the thrifty housewife, including how to sew old stockings inside the seat of pants to extend their life. There are newspaper cuttings too, including the hilarious 'Beautifying society disbands – apathy is blamed', possibly from the *Hawke's Bay Herald-Tribune*, as well as lots of Ian Gordon's 'Language' columns from the *Listener*, in which he explains the etymology of 'enormity', or 'shortbread'.

This stuff isn't terribly useful to me, but I like the little indicators of class and economic circumstance and the reminders of Grandma's love of language. I'm struck by the evidence, in the increasing spideriness of the shopping lists, of her ageing and decline.

And amid the dross, gold: a large bundle of Grandma's mail, including letters from Dad from the late 1950s on, and another smaller bundle of Dad's papers, including hire-purchase receipts, newspaper clippings about himself, and some letters.

It's ridiculous that these receipts have been kept so long, but I'm still glad to learn that on the 24th of November 1961 my parents bought a second-hand piano for £65 plus £7/4/– interest and 14/– insurance and stamp duty, and paid it off at £3/16/– a month. That's our piano, *my* piano, the piano with a sticky high E which I practised on for 15 years – though, by the time I got to it, it was a semitone flat and couldn't be tuned back up because the frame was cracked.

Dad's notebook of cash outgoings for a few months in 1983 triggers memory of things I've not thought about for decades: the advent of plastic hexagonal (or were they pentagonal?) milk tokens that you could leave at the gate with the empty bottles instead of the coins that sometimes proved too tempting to passing schoolkids; the time Dad took Anna and me to see *Casablanca* and told us he'd always thought Mum looked like Ingrid Bergman (but he'd *kill* us if we told her); my new school shoes bought on layby – frumpy Charlie Browns rather than the cooler but pricier Nomads. There's a tiny time-travelling thrill just looking at the prices: *New Zealand Herald* 20¢, loaf of bread 78¢, butter 96¢.

My favourite find, though, is one of the few letters to Dad from his father Ernest. It's written in November 1965, five years before I was born, and reveals something I didn't know but which hardly surprises me: my parents came close to defaulting on the mortgage on our house in Torbay.

Grandad sounds pretty angry that his idiot son, 30 years old and with a wife, four young children (so far), a fulltime teaching job and a promising sideline as a publisher, is asking for a loan Grandad can't really spare, and yet . . .

> I do not want to see you lose your house thus the cheque. I have had to get an overdraft as I never had that amount available.

It's the next sentence, though, that reveals the real distance between father and son, between the hard-working National-voting provincial baker and the long-haired left-leaning literature-loving Bohemian who sprang cuckoo-like from his nest.

> I feel that if you had looked after the interior of the house in the way of wallpaper and paint on walls and kept the garage in repair you would have no trouble in raising a loan. It is not much sense me rubbing it in but the idea of letting children do what they like in the way of scribbling on walls and tearing wallpaper does not pay dividends.

Grandad obviously makes a sound financial point, but just as obviously he's never considered how much fun it might be to be a child and to be allowed to draw on the walls. His son, however, has.

The rest of the bundle looks promising too – chatty letters from Dad to his folks about the garden and chooks and children, documents that pin a fragmentary memory to a particular time and place, some intriguingly intimate letters from a woman who appears to be a family friend. I scribble some notes and put the most interesting stuff in a folder. Before I start writing this thing in earnest, though, there's somewhere else I need to look.

In 1983, the year I turned 13, Dad's quarterly *Islands* hadn't seen a new issue in two-and-a-half years. He was desperate to get it up and running again but the journal, and by extension our family, had completely run out of money. He wanted to send letters of apology to all the subscribers waiting for their magazine, but reckoned he couldn't afford the postage.

Eggs, chickens and vegetables from our garden, supplemented by Dad's occasional wages from relief teaching and freelance editing, kept us from going hungry, but he couldn't pay printers with eggs and silverbeet (though he may well have considered it – I remember him defraying a dentist's bill by taking in a tray of eggs fresh from the fowl-run).

Then someone came to his rescue. Jim Traue, chief librarian of the Alexander Turnbull Library in Wellington, wrote to Dad to say he'd heard of his financial troubles, and to repeat an offer he'd made years earlier to buy the *Islands* archive – manuscripts, proofs, incoming mail and carbon copies of the letters Dad wrote back – for the Turnbull's collection of unpublished papers.

After some hand-wringing – he'd always wanted to gift everything to the library rather than sell it – Dad agreed, and by the end of the year the library had paid a first instalment of $2000. With that in the bank, plus some funds rustled up from other sources, *Islands* could rise again.

As it happened, Dad didn't hold up his end of the transaction until 14 years later, when a library staffer drove up to Auckland and fetched a fraction of the literary detritus that filled a room and a half of his house, and took it back to the Turnbull to be filed. Later still, in November 2014, I would take a couple of weeks off work and fly to the capital to take a look.

I don't know quite what I'm expecting, but if flicking through the 100 or so letters Melissa dropped off was dipping my toe into archival research, entering the Turnbull is like being thrown overboard. I'm drowning.

Dad's papers were stored for years in teetering stacks of cardboard boxes but for some reason, presumably ease of filing, the library has split them into 350-odd foolscap folders, each containing a sheaf of papers up to 5cm thick. According to the library index, bits of Dad's correspondence also appear in the Turnbull archives of 42 other people.

Each folder must be ordered with a computer booking system before it can be delivered, still chilly from its temperature- and humidity-controlled vault (the librarians wear Swanndris down there), to the front desk of the Katherine Mansfield Reading Room. After surviving decades of silverfish and mould spores and Auckland humidity, after dodging the fate of Dad's two-metre-high stack of old

Listener magazines which one summer were eaten by a colony of wasps and converted into a fearsome hive, Dad's old papers are enjoying a surprisingly safe and comfortable retirement.

I leaf through each folder as fast as I can without distressing the watchful librarians, one of whom tells me off for licking my page-flipping finger. I photograph anything that looks interesting for closer reading later, and Jocelyn, the wonderful librarian who's digging out most of the files, invents an extra identity for me so I can order files twice as fast. Even so I get through just 16 folders on the first day, and take about 200 photos. At this rate I'll never get through it all.

Some files are alphabetical, some are chronological, and others are a bit of both. The upshot is that I'm trying to skim-read four decades of Dad's professional life involving complex, long-running relationships with dozens, maybe hundreds, of people – in near-random order. I'm leaping from the late 1950s to the early 1990s then back to the 60s, then to the 80s. People are alive then dead then dying, then alive once more; Dad is a father of six, of none, of four; he's despairing and inert, he's dynamic and optimistic; he's ready to give things one last shot, he's just getting started. He's doddering, he's young, he's having a midlife crisis.

I'm interested to see what's here, but part of me is hoping I can get away with skimming the lot and jotting down the famous names Dad corresponded with, then be done with it. I want to write an intimate, impressionistic book, not something academic and exhaustive. There must be an English Literature PhD student somewhere who has the time and patience to index this ocean and write a handsomely footnoted history of post-colonialism in mid-century New Zealand literary journals or something.

There are indeed plenty of boring, glanceable documents – discussions with printers about pagination and so on – but many others are too seductive to skim. They're not simply the professional exchanges of an editor with his galaxy of writers, would-be writers, artists, illustrators, academics, subscribers and critics, but also lovely things, consciously well made by people who have a way with words.

Letters frequently start with a grovelling apology for delay ('it is quite disgraceful that I have taken so long . . .') or for the inadequacy of what's to follow ('I wonder if you'll excuse just a short note') followed by a critique of the preceding correspondence ('it was a very pleasant surprise to receive your good letter'), before moving on to business.

There's fond scatological banter ('Dear shithead,' writes James K. Baxter on 22 March 1967, 'With affectionate regards I enclose this pile of crap . . .'). There's literary backbiting ('Have you read Shadbolt's godawful new novel?' a young poet asks); and great sentences: 'I am also writing hard,' says the same poet in 1974, '& am not sure if it's out of anger with myself or with the lumpy world.'

For Dad, the boundary between professional and personal was vanishingly thin, so family updates and intimate revelations share the page with a discussion of grammatical nuance and inadequate character development, or the commissioning of an essay. The carbons of his letters to the novelist Maurice Gee sit alongside an impassioned letter to the Wildlife Branch of the Internal Affairs Department, in which he begs for the return of one of our two tame Canada Geese, which had wandered from our Christchurch property and been relocated by officials to a wildlife park where it was now 'being bullied by a wide selection of geese ducks and swan'. Meanwhile, Dad writes, 'the bird we still have at home is [. . .] obviously pining'.

There are also things in these folders that shouldn't be here at all: my Form Two school report, a poster for a sister's school play, shopping lists on the backs of envelopes, and what look suspiciously like love letters to Dad from two more women who aren't Mum, at points in history when they should have been. Like it or not, I'm going to have to take a look at *everything* in these files.

The library offers up an appetiser within half an hour of my arrival. It's in the archives of Frank Sargeson, the capsicum-growing elder statesmen of New Zealand letters. In March 1978, the month of Sargeson's 75th birthday, Dad turned over an entire edition of *Islands* to a celebration of him: Sargeson stories and novel extracts sat alongside dozens of tributes from fellow writers including C. K. Stead, Bill Manhire and Kevin Ireland. I also find letters between Dad and Janet Frame where she declines to contribute to the issue, despite having 'so many illuminating, de-light-ful, moving memories of knowing Frank'.

There must have been some sort of knees-up to launch the special edition. I don't remember it, but a letter from Dad to Frank a few days later shows I was there.

> Ah, well . . . thank you Frank for putting up with Thursday's hoo-har so graciously. I think it all went very well.
>
> I've just told Karl--& I'm sure you'd appreciate it too--that while Karl was singing the praises of ISLANDS, seven-year-old Adam whispered to Anna, 'Yes, but he's not a very good father'! . . . and laughed like drain this morning when I faced him with this treasonable utterance.

As I read this, 36 years on, I laugh out loud once again (though it's more a stifled 'ha!' – I'm wary of the librarians). I'm well aware that by the time I was 12 or 13 I was taking righteous pleasure in explaining Dad's flaws to him, but I had no idea I was such a traitorous little shit quite so young. I decide, forgivingly, that seven-year-old me was probably just trying to make his sister laugh. I email a cellphone snapshot of the letter to Anna.

Recently I've been trying to remember how Dad's voice sounded and finding it difficult, but 'laughed like [a] drain' has spun a tiny neural cog and for just a moment I almost hear him. This was one of his stock lines, along with describing tired or mascaraed eyes as 'pissholes in the snow' or saying his daughters' nail polish made their fingers look like they'd been 'dipped in blood'. If you asked him where he was going, he was always going to 'build a wigwam for a goose's bridle' or 'to see a man about a dog'. Ask why, and you'd learn that 'Y's a crooked letter, and your nose is not much better'.

Seeing Sargeson's name reminds me of the day Frank spent at our house in Torbay, when I was about 12. He was dying of cancer and mostly sat quietly in a chair with his stick next to him and our cat Haydn on his knee, but at some point his catheter bottle needed emptying and Dad ceremonially conveyed it outside to empty onto the lemon tree.

In almost every folder that I open, something sparks. In Sargeson's inbound mail is a note from my mother, written in 1980, thanking Frank for the gift of $43 that paid for her new pair of spectacles. I don't remember her getting new specs – why would I? – and what strikes me about this note isn't the words but the handwriting. Since her stroke Mum has been able to write only with her left hand, painstakingly printing each shaky letter, but this is her old right-handed pre-stroke script, an elegant looping cursive which I've always found beautiful but difficult to read. And *CLICK* – I'm three years old, perhaps four, and I'm trying to read a page of a letter that Mum is halfway through writing, but all I can see is coils of black ink looping across the page like broken springs, and I hear myself saying, 'This is silly – it doesn't say anything at all', and I find a pen of my own to demonstrate that I can write the same meaningless coils. One of the adults in the room is laughing indulgently at me, and I feel indignant.

If I pause the memory I can look around and see the whole moment. The oval kauri dining table is behind me, and I'm standing in front of the high divan next to the white-framed casement windows that you have to jolt with your palm to open because of the swollen wood, and through them you can see the branches of the tree growing in the little cracked-concrete courtyard outside.

I find letters about Dad's brief stint as acting editor at Auckland University Press, during which time he spruced himself up into an approximation of a conventional pen-pusher – and I can see him at the bathroom sink with a pair of scissors, cutting his own crooked fringe and trimming his beard down from enormous to simply large, leaving hairs all over the bench which will really annoy Mum, and early in the morning, before Anna and I have even had breakfast, he's heading out the door, still Dad, but somehow all wrong, too posh in his grey polyester walk shorts and calf-high socks and a shirt with a collar, looking so thoroughly scrubbed he's rubbed some of himself off.

There's a burnt matchstick hiding between two 1985 letters – and I can see the ash-tipped cigarette in his hand, the red soft-pack of 10 Pall Mall Plain in his shirt pocket, the yellow nicotine staining his calloused hands. I remember the sweet, comforting tobacco smell that permeated his office and clothes and hair and skin, and the exciting moment one day when he put a spent match back into the matchbox without checking it was fully out, and the box exploded into flame in his hands.

There's no bin near my table in the reading room, so I hand the matchstick to a librarian, Paul, when I return the folder at day's end. When I return to the same folder the next morning, the matchstick has been carefully re-filed with the letters.

I sit and flick and snap and scribble and stand and fetch and sit and flick and snap, hour after hour. At times the skim-reading becomes hypnotic and the meanings of words drift away, leaving me to notice the shapes and colours: flimsy blue aerogrammes, blurry carbon copies, chirpy postcards with writing that overshoots the last line and runs across the bottom and up the side, shouty yellow telegrams with their messages about a printing delay or an urgent correction printed in anxious capitals on strips of white tickertape glued to the page.

I decode the angular red letters of Dad's occasional handwritten letters, and note the sudden switch in his outgoing carbon copies from a classic seriffed typewriter face to an anaemic sans serif in mid-1975, when a writer friend gave him her old Smith-Corona Galaxie Deluxe, replacing the near-dead machine Dad had bought 20-odd years earlier with his pay from a holiday job washing sheepskins at the Tomoana Freezing Works. And in 1980 the Galaxie too was replaced, by an IBM Selectric with crisply uniform letters and super-modern interchangeable font golfballs. At night, as I fell asleep, I would hear the loud electric clunk of each letter through the wall between his office and my bedroom. He used the Selectric till the 1990s, by which time he and everyone else was switching to word processors, with their reckless profusion of typefaces and Zapf Dingbat pointy fingers.

As the days pass and my camera memory fills up, the thrill of finding yet another funny or useful or evocative document is replaced with a low-grade panic that I'll never get through all this material before my fortnight's up – and even if I do I'll never be able to filter it down into something readable.

A few months ago, I was at a writing workshop where Peter Wells talked about a history he was working on, based initially around five family letters written over the course of a century. I'm starting to think that five letters might be the right amount of material. Perhaps, like the cartographers in the Borges story who make a 1:1-scale map of their empire, I could spend the next 40 years publishing this archive online, each day posting the documents from one day in the past.

Eventually I get a grip, and realise that ingesting so much material in a single gulp has an advantage: it helps me see the bigger patterns. I imagine laying out all the letters in chronological order and assigning each an emotional colour – anxious red, cheerful orange, serious blue, gloomy grey – then watching the palette shift and change over the decades: from the gangle-limbed vigour of the late 1950s, to the bright, brassy excitement and busyness of the 1960s with new jobs and a new family, to the vivid yet spiky 1970s when his career was soaring, and to the 1980s, which started out overcast and only got darker.

I already know first-hand about the anxieties of the 1980s,

but what I'm surprised to discover is that even when his career and family life and his physical and mental health were at their peak, Dad was always running hard to stand still, always on the brink of calamity. There was *never* enough time or money or energy. He was *always* behind with the gardening, with his bills, with house repairs, with the latest magazine deadline. The surprising thing isn't that he eventually ran out of puff; it's that he didn't do so much earlier.

Yet there were always moments of grace. In July 1974 Dad wrote to the academic and writer James Bertram about his ambitions and fears for *Islands*, then in its third year. Subscriptions were up and the next edition might sell a healthy 1700 copies, but as usual it was a struggle to do the job as well as he wanted. He was glad, though, to be living back in Auckland:

> We're feeling a bit squeezed here but I have moments of quite intense happiness based on warmth, and beach and hills and green--it's quite odd and only underlines, for me, the purgatory that Chch amounted to for so much of the time. More time --to work to read, to visit, to think--is all I crave. Some hope.

I don't quite know why – something to do with those 'moments of quite intense happiness' – but as I read this letter in the library my eyes fill with tears, and I have to stop and sit for quite a while.

There's one folder, a miscellany of correspondence of 1988–90, from when *Islands* was folding for the second time. His family were barely talking to him, and he was skint and miserable.

This folder is all incoming (and I suspect unanswered) mail: cheques from *Islands* subscribers never banked because there wasn't a magazine to send in return; polite letters from libraries requesting information on the status of their subscription; even politer letters from writers wondering if they might have their submissions back ('If circumstances have forced you to lay Islands to rest permanently I wonder if you could let me know so that I might offer the Soap sequence elsewhere,' writes poet James Norcliffe).

All this is sitting tidily in front of me, pieces of paper collected in a clean beige foolscap folder with a computer-printed label – 'MS-Papers-8988-199' – but it's actually a portrait of a man falling over.

In the Katherine Mansfield Reading Room times passes quickly and, for the most part, very quietly, apart from the *shlunk* of my camera shutter and the riffle of pages. One morning a librarian gives a piercing scream after finding an earwig in her hair. She flings it to the floor, stamps on it four times and has an intense discussion with her colleague about whether they should report the incident to Conservation, a decision which turns largely on whether it came to work with her from her garden or originated somewhere in the library. Another day an elderly couple – the husband deaf and the wife shouting – keep the whole room entertained as they try to track down the right edition of *The Grey River Argus.*

I meet a friendly freelance researcher who knows a lot about lighthouses. I exchange pleasantries with an anarchist, slightly notorious since police covertly filmed her allegedly training in the use of Molotov cocktails, who is researching an anti-war project and has a piece of tape covering the webcam of her laptop. I compare notes with the historian Rachel Barrowman, who is nearing completion of the biography of Maurice Gee that she started a decade ago. Moss and Dad were friends, so we've been reading some of the same letters between them, but it's pretty obvious that Rachel is doing a drastically more thorough job than I'm planning.

I learn that Dad's stuff takes up about seven linear metres of shelving in the Turnbull's vault. The full unpublished manuscripts collection stretches to 10km. There must be a lot of powerful secrets lurking in there. I ask a librarian if people ever freak out in the reading room – burst into tears or shout in anger as they come across a love letter, or a bequest that was never honoured.

'No,' she says. 'Not really.'

After two weeks of cramming, I'm waiting for my flight at Wellington airport. During a big push in the last couple of days, I've sighted all but a handful of Dad's folders, and those were only page proofs and typescripts, so hopefully I've missed nothing important. I've got 4500 photos on my computer and screeds of notes to help me navigate them when I return and read them properly. I'm knackered.

After checking in for my flight I open my laptop to rattle off brief thank-you emails to Jocelyn and her colleagues, and to the friends who've put me up. Then I stop, and shut the lid.

Whitcoulls has just one postcard design on sale – a wretchedly ugly Photoshopped montage of Auckland beaches, including one photo I'm pretty sure is Waiake, the beach nearest our house in Torbay, where Dad found some of those moments of intense happiness. I buy four cards for 50 cents.

My handwriting is so atrophied by a lifetime of computers that it's barely legible, but I scrawl something friendly and inane on each, and drop them into the postbox. Someone's got to keep on writing letters.

4. Woodspring Cottage

One day you notice that it's been forever since you last rode on your father's shoulders, or chewed on your mother's thumb because you liked the feel of the strong, spongy flesh between your teeth, or squeezed into the warm-bed nook between the two of them. The firm knowledge that you own your parents' bodies as much as your own is fading – but it never quite passes. You never forget their smell and taste, their skin and the bones and muscles just beneath. You know the backs of their hands.

My father was an adventure playground. His front, from shin to collarbone, was a wall to climb as you leant back into the belay of his arms. You could climb halfway then flip backwards to the ground with your arms turned inside out, or go all the way up, clambering around on his head and shoulders before settling into the saddle of his neck and grasping handfuls of black hair for reins, pausing only to reassure yourself of the egg-sized lump just above his left ear, from the time he was knocked unconscious by the head of a sledgehammer that flew off its handle. Equally, you could steer the horse by tugging at his jug ears, the only convincing aspect of his alleged resemblance to Prince Charles.

When he was driving his baby-blue Ford Transit van, those ears were mysteriously connected to the windscreen: if you crept up from behind (no seatbelts in the back) and twisted the left one, water would spray across the screen; twist the right and the wipers would sweep across and back. Even after I'd located the foot-operated pump in the driver's footwell – a small black rubber hemisphere which reminded me of the diaphragm Mum kept in a plastic box in the cupboard under the bathroom sink – Dad managed to convince me that he wasn't cheating.

He also had a magic cardigan which, if you turned away for a moment to allow him to put it on, made him invisible. My faith in these mystical abilities is as close as I ever got to religion.

His clenched fist was a safe to unlock, but even if I could get one finger unfurled it would snap back as I tried the next. When we wrestled on the couch I'd abandon myself to the joy of total violence, confident that however hard I tried I couldn't bend or break or bruise him.

In the sea, he was a diving platform and inflatable toy. He was extraordinarily buoyant – I wonder if his mild pigeon chest gave him a greater than average lung capacity, though I'm not sure that's medically plausible – and he would lie back with arms folded behind his head then pretend to be annoyed when, inevitably, one of his children leapt aboard and sank him.

He was seldom happier than when in water. The Transit

smelt of dog and salt and sometimes of the iodine seaweed we'd collect for the garden from Long Bay Beach after a big storm. When the surf was up he'd lead me into the waves with one of our iceblock-shaped surfboards and we'd catch the wave, stacked up like a liquorice allsort – a layer of polystyrene, a layer of Dad, a layer of me – scudding all the way in till we juddered to a halt on the wet sand.

Most evenings he'd have a long bath, run so hot that if you planned to get in with him you had to start by sitting on the edge, scalding socks of scarlet onto your feet and calves until the water had cooled or your body had acclimatised. Even after we were too old to be sharing, his baths remained sociable – he'd lie bright red and sweating under the rising steam, chest hair wafting like seagrass, a draped facecloth modestly floating in the vicinity of his balls and intriguingly circumcised penis, reading a hardback crime novel from the library as the rest of the family shuttled in to wash hands and brush teeth.

When I was still small enough I'd join him in the shower to wash off the salt and sand after a swim, and he'd lift me all the way up to the nozzle, where I'd be amazed at how hot the water was up there and how great the pressure.

My second-earliest memory is of being on an infinitely wide beach at low tide. I start to cross the sand to the distant water before noticing the ground is covered in millions of little red insect things. I can't move without standing on one. I start to scream. Dad is suddenly there, sweeping me up in his arms before carrying me across the carpet of stranded lobster krill and into the sea.

This was in Nelson in early 1974, a few months after my third birthday. The Dudding family was in the middle of a six-week sightseeing migration from Christchurch to Auckland, travelling and sleeping in the Transit, which was then near-new. My sisters remember the krill, too, and how they used our Frisbee to scoop the beasts off the sand in their hundreds and throw them at each other.

My very first memory is from a few weeks earlier again. Dad and I went to collect the van from a vehicle workshop in Christchurch, where it had been fitted with a bed, cooker and awning. I remember the sound of power tools, the smell of sawdust, a feeling of adventure.

For anything earlier, for all the Christchurch years, I have to turn to the memories of my sisters and family friends.

First though, an explanation: what were we doing in Christchurch anyway?

By the mid-1960s Robin Dudding, his wife Lois and their four daughters Rachel, Ruth, Melissa and Natasha were living in Torbay on Auckland's then-remote North Shore. Robin was nominally a fulltime schoolteacher, but much of his time and energy was spent editing the occasional literary journal *Mate*, a younger, brasher, cooler alternative to the highly regarded but relentlessly highbrow literary quarterly *Landfall*, which was published by Christchurch's Caxton Press and edited by its co-founder Charles Brasch.

When Brasch quit as editor in 1966, he recommended that *Mate*'s ambitious young editor be offered the job. So in August that year the Duddings moved to Christchurch, where Dad took up the dual position of editor of *Landfall* and of Caxton Press. Children kept arriving – Anna in 1967, me in 1970 – then in 1972 Robin was fired from Caxton (more on that excitement later) so he launched his own magazine,

Islands, taking with him most of *Landfall*'s writers, mana and support (including that of Brasch).

He stayed in Christchurch for the next year and a half, producing *Islands* from our home, but both he and Mum were pining for the relative warmth, literal and figurative, of Auckland where their little house in Torbay was waiting for them, albeit slightly worse for wear after seven-and-a-half years of tenants. In January 1974 they packed the van, including a typewriter so that Dad could work on the next edition of *Islands* en route, and we said goodbye to 15 Barnes Road, Redwood.

Just as we were about to leave, Dad trotted back to the house. To the right of the front door was a wooden plaque that said 'Woodspring Cottage' in a fancy font. He prised it off and carried it back to the van. We all posed for a final photo – Mum and Dad and six kids and an Alsatian-Labrador cross called Lady Emma Hamilton Dudding, plus a handful of neighbours and friends there to wave us off – then we all climbed in, Dad started the engine and we started driving north.

It's pure suburbia now, but in the late 1960s Redwood, five miles north of central Christchurch, was still on the edge of the city. At Barnes Road, where the burbs merged into farmland and orchards, close to the near-dry Styx River, the Duddings created some sort of pastoral utopian fantasy.

At least that's how it seemed to Bill Manhire, a poet 10 years Dad's junior who came to talk literature but ended up a good friend. Manhire remembers our home as a place where things happened outdoors rather than indoors, where there were dogs and cats and chickens and geese, and the garden was abundant even if money was very tight. It seemed an enviable set-up, a stand against suburban New Zealand, a tiny, single-family commune with a literary guru as benign patriarch, a fecund earth-mother keeping everyone fed, and a tribe of unruly girls. On one of his visits Manhire, who had a repertoire of minor magic tricks, demonstrated how he could apparently bend a spoon without damaging it, leaving such a devastating impression on the Dudding daughters that they set about mutilating every spoon in the cutlery drawer.

Come up the drive at Barnes Road, says writer Patrick Evans, and all these girls of six and eight and ten would appear and jump on you like monkeys, and demand to be taken places.

For Evans, raised in 'fantastically conservative' Christchurch by snobbish English parents, the place was bucolic and countercultural, with its ping-pong table which served as dining table and its bookshelves made from wooden planks and empty DB beer bottles.

Evans came to the fortnightly Friday evening soirées at Barnes Road, where Mum made big pots of curry and brown rice with toasted coconut and sliced banana and raisins as condiments, and the girls would wander around with bowls of roasted peanuts, topping up glasses from the bottles that would later become bookshelves, and Dad would be in the large front room that he used as an office, surrounded by writers and poets and artists – the established ones, the coming ones, the would-bes – somehow holding court even though he spoke softly and didn't actually say much. There'd be some drunkenness but these weren't wild saturnalia, just big gatherings with music and lots of good feeling and plenty of literary talk without it being stuffy.

Evans says 1970 was the year dope came to Christchurch, mostly via the Americans stationed at the international airport for the long-running Antarctic mission Operation Deep Freeze. If you wanted to buy good, cheap drugs you'd just head to the airbase – and some of them found their way to the Barnes Road gatherings. The dope-smokers would end up down the side of the house, wedged in like passengers in a bus at rush hour, handing around pieces of wet paper with dazed faces.

Dad's papers from those years show that both before and after being fired from Caxton he was working long hours, worrying about money, struggling to meet deadlines, and fretting about work keeping him from his family and vice versa. Yet my sisters don't recall such stresses inside the Barnes Road bubble.

They remember the Friday parties: a day of Mum vacuuming and cleaning and cooking, then loud music on the record player – Beatles, Dylan, Simon and Garfunkel, the Animals – as the guests arrived carrying their bottles of beer. Anna, youngest of the five girls, remembers playing under the table among the feet of the adults talking above.

Another big event was Wednesday craft night. When Mum went to her night class, still chipping away at the arts degree she'd started before marriage, Dad would run the household for the evening. With a magician's flourish he'd reach up to one of the high cupboards in the living room and bring down treasures: modelling clay, pens and paper and glue, cotton wool, eggshells that had been crushed and coloured pink and blue for sprinkling over a glue drawing, and uncrushed eggshells that could be made into miniature igloos. On these nights, Mum's sternly wholesome food rules were overturned.

Instead of mince and boiled cabbage, dinner might be tinned spaghetti or mashed potatoes and chops, with stewed apple topped with a square of baked puff pastry for pudding, perhaps even ice cream.

When Mum was off having another baby or visiting relatives, Dad would again run the ship and break the rules. Instead of Mum's awful homemade wholemeal bread (so dense and sour the round loaves often ended up being used as Frisbees), he'd make school sandwiches using proper shop bread – one side brown and the other wonderfully, joyously white. He'd also sneak in little packets of chips and raisins.

Compared to the two-bedroomed Torbay home that came before and after, Barnes Road seemed huge – half an acre of land, four or five bedrooms, a porch, a large living room and a vast kitchen with its own fire, where the girls would cluster around as Dad read aloud in the evening. Natasha remembers the night Dad was reading from *The Hobbit* and she climbed onto a wooden soapbox balanced on its end to get closer. When the box collapsed a nail tore a gash across her knee. A sticking plaster was found and *The Hobbit* continued, but she's still got the scar.

Woodspring Cottage was always cold – there were numerous fireplaces, but even with your feet brushing the flames the rest of you would be freezing. Once, the two youngest girls stuffed the sitting-room woodburner so full of paper it fell back out, setting fire to the carpet and a couch. That was the woodburner that Natasha and Melissa would leap from, arms aflutter, whenever 'If You Want to Be a Bird' played on our LP of the *Easy Rider* soundtrack.

Hours were spent playing and building things on the banks of the Styx, with its old trees and leaf litter and a hollow tree stump that was just the right size and shape to be a long-drop toilet, so was used as such. The Barnes Road property itself was full of exciting trees – the huge elm at the bottom of the garden with a hut halfway up it, the psoriatic lacebark that could be used to climb the garage roof, the fruit trees, the yews lining the driveway. When the council put in a footpath for the first time, they wanted to chop down a cabbage tree out the front but Dad persuaded them not to, then wrote a note thanking them for their part in creating 'the crookedest and most attractive footpath in the county'. He and Mum spent weeks lobbying a next-door neighbour not to cut down their giant walnut, but failed. Mum went out to argue with the axemen on the day of execution then came home and wept piteously – a rare and distressing thing.

Child-minding was often delegated to the older girls, who used it as an opportunity to conduct experiments. Rachel and Ruth (numbers one and two) led weekend walks along the nearby railway, placing ear to metal to check for trains. They blindfolded Melissa (number three) and guided her across the bridge over the Styx with their voices alone, and she only fell off once. It was Melissa, too, who got a nasty bite on the chest from one of the semi-wild Shetland ponies on the field backing onto ours.

Natasha (number four) and Anna (number five) persuaded me (number six) to dial 111 and use all my swearwords; the police rang back and instructed Mum to tell the children off, but it's not clear if she did. I'm told Natasha also persuaded me, aged two, to ask Mum what a 'wanker' was. Boringly for Natasha and Anna, watching from around the corner, Mum just told me. The most disgusting piece of inter-sibling betrayal was the time one child extruded a tiny raisin-sized poo on the front porch, and a second told a third it was in fact a raisin and popped it in her mouth.

When I arrived in November 1970, first boy after five girls, the scope for experimentation only broadened. The girls vied for the right to dandle their fat baby brother, or to wheel him around in the pram wearing their old dresses so they could trick school friends into believing they had another baby sister. They also discovered that if they wiggled the baby's penis with a teddy bear it would, most exotically, stand up.

Sibling terrorism aside, it felt special to be one of the Dudding girls. There was no TV, but that was by choice and you could always watch *Sonny and Cher* or *The Carol Burnett Show* at a friend's house. There wasn't a lot of money, but that felt like a minor virtue rather than something to be embarrassed about, and there always seemed to be enough for music lessons and sports trips and second-hand pushbikes. For a long while there was a large hole in the kitchen floor that didn't get repaired, but that was kind of funny, and the girls would proudly tell the story of how one day Mum lost her temper with someone – perhaps her husband, but more likely a child – and threw a frying pan at the kitchen wall, leaving an interesting hole you could still see.

Dad seemed to be always working – away at Caxton, or in his office at home, or sweating in the vegetable garden with a hoe or a spade while wearing only underpants – yet somehow he was always available too. He led backyard games of softball and cricket, and of minigolf using hockey sticks as putters and buried tin cans for holes. He created a table-tennis handicapping system that family members and visitors were obliged to join, with paper nametags that moved up and down a cardboard ladder of his own devising (this was still running by the time I left home in 1991). And though Mum was the principal day-to-day child-wrangler, Dad made a point of taking trips alone with each daughter – a roadtrip to Dunedin to visit the Manhires, to Hawke's Bay to visit his folks, or a simple outing to a movie or ice skating or the greyhounds.

For Rose Beauchamp, the friend who talked at Dad's funeral about arriving at Barnes Road to find Mum reading up a tree, the Christchurch Duddings of the early 1970s seemed to demonstrate it was possible to interweave 'serious' creative goals – being a writer or artist or musician or a literary editor, say – with more basic, biological forms of creativity: growing vegetables, planting trees, breastfeeding naked in the sunshine, keeping chooks, raising children who were encouraged to talk at the dinner table and allowed to draw on the wallpaper. It was a template she and her husband Ian Wedde wanted to follow.

Before then it had seemed to Rose that you had to choose; that the creative life necessarily involved hard drinking and drug-taking and, probably, being male; that if you were a woman and wanted to be an artist you should probably abandon your children and certainly not consider mothering itself as a creative act. Yes, says Rose, there was a division of labour down traditional lines at Barnes Road – Robin in his office with books, Lois the kitchen queen – but there was a mutual exchange of influence and respect.

The initial connection between Duddings and Weddes was that Dad was publishing Ian's writing, but after the Weddes moved to Port Chalmers in Dunedin, where Ian was the Robert Burns fellow, the two families fell rather in love with each other, remaining so even after respective migrations to Auckland and Wellington. With all those births behind her, Lois was a fount of baby-related wisdom when Rose started having children of her own ('eat like a navvy' when breastfeeding, and so on). For Ian, the house in Christchurch became 'a kind of haven – and that's where I learnt to grow tomatoes, and learnt to like a chook, and came to love a dog'. When Emma had pups, Dad bundled two of them into shipping crates and put them on a train to Port Chalmers, and informed the Weddes that they were now dog-owners, ready or not.

I've been talking to my mother about Dad in one way or another all my life, but with a book in mind I try to get a bit more professional about it – preparing questions in advance, setting a recorder on the table, talking less and listening to her more.

It's slow work. Tongue-tied by her stroke, Mum can take a long time to say little. Once, though, she tells me she chose Dad over other suitors not so much because of any physical appeal, but because 'I thought he'd make a good father'. Another time, when we're discussing how she and Dad never hit us children (well, almost never), she says she always thought of Dad's own father Ernest as a cruel man who bullied his children and, like just about everyone else of that time, hit them. When Dad was old enough and big enough, Mum says, he went against his father in every way he possibly could, and that included a gentler approach to children.

I never much liked Grandad when Dad dragged us to Hastings to visit his folks. Ernest's main mode for connecting with his grandchildren was a repertoire of practical jokes that ended with him hitting you on the nose after inviting you to 'smell the cheese' on his outstretched palm or pointing out the 'gravy on your shirt'. He'd offer you a 'dry shave', where he'd drag his cheek against yours, scraping your face raw with his stubble. He was also a master of the finger-lock, where you couldn't pull away your little finger without causing yourself excruciating pain. I hate that stuff.

Then again, a few days after I've written those last few sentences, my sister Ruth emails to ask me if I remember how when slicing bread at the table Ernest would ask us who wanted the baker's kiss – the best, softest slice, formed when you tear apart a loaf made from two pieces of dough risen in a single tin – and whoever said yes would get an actual kiss from him, because he was a baker, see! I quite like the sound of that one, but no, I don't remember it.

I'll learn more about Ernest, though, when I fly to New Plymouth to talk to Dad's younger brother, Ian.

5. Tripe on Friday

SUNDAY WAS roast, Monday cold meat with salad. Tuesday was sausage, Wednesday chopped steak. Thursday was stew – so Ernest could eat it with a spoon in bed as he rested up before his all-night shift at the bakery – and Friday was fish, or something exotic like tripe or pigs' trotters. Saturday was bacon and eggs. And every day there was pudding – a steamed pudding or fruit with custard, or on Sundays something cooked in the oven with the roast, like rice pudding or sago.

My uncle Ian is sitting in an armchair in his kitchen, dredging up what he can of his childhood and Dad's. He wasn't sure he liked the idea at first, but he's warming to it.

Ian has never resembled his older brother. He's got the deep eyesockets, broad jaw and sloping forehead of their father Ernest (who always reminded me of Hugh Lofting's illustrations of Dr Dolittle). Robin was taller, darker, slim-faced, narrow-jawed. Ian is 77, born a year-and-a-half after Dad, and he's lovely: a gentle, self-deprecating guy with a scratchy giggle. He has recently retired as town planner with the New Plymouth council, and is far smarter than he claims to be.

I'm at the kitchen table typing as he talks. My aunt Gail is on the edge of the conversation, filling in gaps and offering alternative interpretations. Over a long afternoon and then the following morning, they tell me stories, as brilliant sun and heavy rain take turns beating at the window.

Ian and Gail are the family genealogists, so they can talk about the Lincolnshire Duddings and the Birmingham Hintons (upper and lower middle-class respectively), about the Doggetts and Wealleans of London (both thoroughly working class) and Elizabeth Jackson of Macclesfield (background and social status unclear). They can trace the various arrivals from the 1870s on, and the planting of shallow roots in small-town New Zealand – Tirau, Midhurst, Kawhia, Otorohanga, Hunterville, Bulls, Rangitikei, Oxford, Kaiapoi, Waimakariri – where the ancestors ran a store, managed a boarding house, drove a stagecoach, operated a river punt, reared Lincolnshire sheep, raised children.

Charles Henry Dudding (my great-great-grandfather) was an alcoholic who fell in a river drunk and drowned. His son Horatio was an alcoholic too. In Bulls, the Wealleans family lost mother, father and eldest daughter from separate causes in a single month, so 14-year-old Liz raised the two oldest boys while the other six siblings, including my great-great-grandmother May Emily, were sent on the *Stormbird* to Burnham Industrial School in the South Island. One boy died. When some of the others returned north as adults they erased the orphanage years, claiming they'd been born in Wales.

The stories eventually converge on schoolteacher Winifred Jessie Hinton and baker's son Ernest Charles Dudding, who grew up in Stratford below the eastern slopes of Mount Taranaki, or Mount Egmont as they knew it. They met through Bible class and married years later, when Ernest was 23 and Winifred 29 (though on the marriage certificate they gave their ages as 24 and 26). What I'm really interested in, though, is what happened next, after Winifred and Ernest moved east to Hastings, where Ernest went into partnership with another baker and where Winifred bore three children – Ngaire in 1931, Robin in 1935, Ian in 1937.

When the Hawke's Bay earthquake struck in 1931, the mezzanine floor of Ernest's bakehouse, where the flour was stored, collapsed. At the house he and Winifred were renting in Plassey Street, all the jars of sauce and preserves fell from the cupboards and smashed. But New Zealand's biggest natural disaster of the 20th century left them otherwise unscathed. A year or two later they bought a large section in the same street and built the family home that lasted them a lifetime.

The Duddings were comfortable – they had a fridge before most families in the street – but careful. Veggies and fruit and eggs came from the garden and substantial fowl-run, and day-old bread and pastries from the bakery, though it irked young Robin that they were never allowed anything fresh. The only alcohol ever in the house was a bottle of something for the Christmas cake; after watching his father and grandfather drink and gamble their families into poverty, Ernest was teetotal all his life. When he had a bottle forced on him at a Volunteer Fire Brigade party after the war, he quietly emptied his beer into a pot plant.

Plassey Street was built on routine. Ernest's bakery shifts, dinners and puddings you could predict by the day of the week, school rugby and chores on Saturday (boys outside with Father, Ngaire inside with Mother) and the seventh day for Sunday School and a long walk with Mother, or perhaps a game of tennis on the family's grass court.

Ngaire was off to university before Ian started high school, and the boys were often thrown together. When hostilities broke out, Ian – younger, a weakling, unconfident – usually came off worse. Robin shot him in the eye with a homemade bow and arrow; a shard of glass lodged in Ian's leg when they were playing catch with glass bulbs from the kitchen oven; a furious Ian had to be hauled away from a laughing Robin after a scrap escalated from fists to pieces of firewood.

But they got on well enough. When Ian started school he inherited Robin's rhyming nickname, Spud. They both helped Ernest build a garden shed. For a while they went out running together.

Raising the girl was Mother's job and raising the boys was Father's. Winifred wanted Ngaire, who was brainy and dux of her school, to go to university, and she did. But Ernest, who'd left school at 12 to work in his drunk father's bakery, wanted his sons to take trade rather than academic classes at high school. Ian and Robin each protested when the time came, and with some intervention from Winifred they eventually got their way. It was the only time Ian ever stood up to his father. Ian claims he was too dumb for university, though, so took a surveying cadetship. Robin was smarter but still started work straight from Sixth Form, as a cadet with the *Hawke's Bay Herald-Tribune*.

Ian agrees with my mother's impression of Ernest as a bully. He was pleasant enough if you went his way but swift to anger if you didn't. Sometimes, for no reason, he'd tease you until you were so upset you'd say something disrespectful, then he'd properly lose his temper and give you a hiding. He could hold a grudge, too. Before leaving Stratford he'd had a falling-out over money with his brother Ray, himself something of a drinker, at the bakehouse they ran together, and they never spoke again. In Hastings, Ernest blanked Winifred's brother Herb for several years after Herb allegedly swindled him out of the earnings from a vanload of cakes.

Although Ernest could be mean, it was Winifred who was the more enthusiastic whacker of children. If you didn't come in when you were asked, or hadn't done something you should have, or were caught fibbing, or were in trouble at school, she'd reach for her old schoolteacher's leather strap, which she kept in the kitchen for inside use; or one of her switches – branches of willow or similar stored above the wood-box, for easy access out of doors.

Winifred was academically bright, independent, determined – a conqueror of hills and a pioneering lady driver. The car she bought herself from her teaching salary in the 1920s was Stratford's first Baby Austin. But her single-mindedness could look like heartlessness. Ian remembers one of Winifred's hill-walks where Robin climbed a steep slope despite being warned not to and got stuck halfway up. Robin was 9 or 10 and screaming for help, but he'd been warned, so Winifred led the rest of the family on and Robin was still there when they returned the same way two hours later.

Winifred exerted rigid control over the family's social world. School friends weren't welcome at Plassey Street, and the children were to hurry back home after school without playing. She didn't much like the idea of Maoris, nor foreigners, including the Italians (and their food) she endured during the

European holiday she and Ernest took in 1967. She wasn't terribly fond even of her Dudding in-laws. Her enthusiasm for other families was reserved almost exclusively for those of her six siblings, and with them you were allowed to have fun – play cards and tennis and go for walks, tell gently off-colour jokes and pull each other's leg, or pop around to Uncle Herb's place on election night to listen to the radio broadcast and cheer on the National Party.

The Duddings of Plassey Street also tuned in for *Dad and Dave* and other radio serials. Winifred liked dance music and the light classics; Ernest liked Mario Lanza and the other tenors but loathed the Andrews Sisters. Each year they went to the local operatic society production, and even though he was terrible at holding a tune, Robin had a part in his school production of *The Mikado*. Apparently the title role was taken by Raymond Hawthorne, future patriarch of the Hawthorne acting dynasty.

Robin was encouraged to write by three of his Hastings High teachers: Miss Miller, Mr Alexander and Mr Mathison. He was discovering Shakespeare, poetry, modernism and girls. Near the end of the Fifth Form he wrote a poem for the school magazine, piquing the interest of a bookish and usually shy girl called Anne Croucher, who sought him out and suggested they start doing their Shakespeare homework together. By the following year they were a couple. They read all the avant-garde writers. He gave her a leather-bound *Complete Shakespeare* for one birthday, a poetry volume for another.

The Duddings were all readers, even if Robin was the only one tackling James Joyce and Virginia Woolf. Ngaire read aloud while Winifred did the dishes. The English sailing adventures of *Swallows and Amazons* were favourites, though Winifred objected to Arthur Ransome calling one of his main characters 'Titty', so Ngaire had to replace it with another name.

Winifred liked light historical drama – Nelle Scanlan's *Pencarrow* family sagas about a pioneering Wellington family, the *Billabong* books by Australian Mary Grant Bruce – and always read past midnight. Ernest liked Westerns. He read the *Auckland Weekly News* cover to cover, as did the children. He also took the *Truth*, but given its salaciousness the children were allowed to read only the cartoon pages in the middle.

They didn't own all that many books – a small bookshelf contained Arthur Mee's children's encyclopaedias, a book of Robert Burns's verse, a copy of *Lorna Doone* and Sir Walter Scott's *Kenilworth* and a few others – but Winifred brought home a pile for everybody from the library each week. She let the children read her books, but Ernest's Westerns were off-limits. There was a solitary Western, *Rustlers' Roost*, in the permanent collection, which Ian spent his childhood yearning to read, but each time he snuck it away Ngaire would 'pimp' him to the adults – 'He's reading that book again!' – and it would be taken off him. Seventy years on, it's now in Ian's own bookshelf, though he never got round to reading it to the end.

While Ngaire and Ian clashed a bit, Ngaire and Robin clashed even more, especially whenever Mother and Father went off to baking conferences and left Ngaire in charge. But the greatest tension in the house was between Robin and Ernest. From the time Robin was 10, they were butting heads. Where Ian would respond to Ernest's bullying simply by doing what he was told, or by pretending to agree and then quietly doing his own thing, for Robin it was always a matter of principle. He'd argue the toss and there'd be shouting on both sides and sometimes Robin would get a hiding.

In his early teens Robin courted trouble by coming home late from his after-school job at the chemist shop. Later, he hung out in the snooker parlours, or drank with his rugby friends – a red rag to teetotal Ernest. The one time Ian saw Robin come home properly drunk, Winifred searched his bag and found a bottle of whisky. She took the bottle into the garden and smashed it with a shovel before burying it and dancing on its grave. Curiously, though, Winifred wouldn't let Ernest lay a finger on Robin that time.

At 16 Robin was a cadet at the *Herald-Tribune* and taking some extramural university papers (which he failed) but still living at home. He caught up with Anne when she was home from training college in Wellington, but by now they were just friends.

At the *Tribune* he covered the usual reporter's gamut – Hawke's Bay's acute cement shortage, the trial of a man charged for drinking a bottle of beer in the street, a local Rotarian calling for a purge of the Hastings Library of filth by the likes of Somerset Maugham, a swan called Gertie that liked to ride on a tractor – but he also manoeuvred himself onto the arts beat, and reviewed theatre and music.

There are gaps in Ian's knowledge of Robin's last few years in Hastings, not least because as they got older the brothers increasingly ignored each other. At 18 Robin went to Auckland for three months' compulsory military training. There, he learnt how to be a light anti-aircraft gunner, and how to have fun. He and another trainee befriended twin sisters Anna and Toni Rutherfurd, Takapuna Grammar schoolgirls who had a car, a frequently parentless house in Milford and lots of friends. Auckland, he was discovering, was a place of warmth and surf and freedom. He returned to Plassey Street and the *Tribune*, but not for long.

I grew up believing the legend that Dad left home straight after a full-blown fist fight with his father that ended with him knocking Ernest to the ground.

One version – perhaps told to me directly by Dad, seeing I can't find anyone else in the family who's heard it – has it that the row began after Ernest found dirty books under Robin's mattress: D. H. Lawrence, James Joyce, maybe Henry Miller. My sister Natasha heard a version where the fist fight started because Dad came home one night drunk.

Ian doesn't recall any fist fight at all, but that doesn't mean the story is completely untrue. In Dad's final year at Plassey Street, Ian was away doing his own military training, and when he returned relations between Ernest and Robin were very tense. Two months later, Robin left home for good.

He was 20 years old. He was returning to Auckland, and from there he planned to save some money and head abroad to see the world, following in the footsteps of a school friend who had crewed fertiliser ships for the free travel.

He made it to Auckland, but then his plans changed. It would be almost half a century before he got his first passport.

6. At the bach

It's a Wednesday, three days before Anzac Day, and I'm alone in a friend's deafeningly quiet bach – actually a large house on a farmland hill near a beautiful empty beach north of Whangarei. I'm writing at the huge dining table. When the kitchen fridge falls quiet all I can hear is the ticking of a clock and the occasional bird conversation from outside, then the short volleys of laptop key clacks whenever I think of something more to write.

I've just had breakfast: two fried eggs on buttered Vogel's toast with some strawberry jam smeared on the half-piece left after the egg was all gone, plus a cup of strong coffee, and I'm enjoying the familiar brief euphoria that follows the perfect breakfast – something to do with blood sugar and caffeine and dopamine receptors, I suppose.

My mind chitters and chirps. I'm enchanted by things I normally don't care about. I've found this can be a good time to get to a keyboard and write, because along with the euphoria and wonder comes a temporary change of heart in the editor who's usually sitting on my shoulder making unhelpful observations – 'Clunky sentence!' or 'Implausible dialogue' and 'Give up now, you're shit'. Instead, the editor seems to have just got back from a boozy lunch. 'You're a genius,' he slurs. 'That linking paragraph is beautifully subtle!' With that kind of encouragement the sentences spew out, and I don't even mind that I'm going to have to read them later in a saner cast of mind and delete most of them.

The truth remains, though, that I don't really know how to write this book. In my day job I've written hundreds of newspaper features, a task which generally consists of agonising over the introductory paragraph then racing against a deadline to write down everything you know about a subject of which you were entirely ignorant two days earlier. But those stories have seldom exceeded 3000 words. I'm not sure I know how to keep things coherent across the longer span of a book, with chapters and everything.

I decided early on that simply telling Dad's story chronologically wasn't the right approach, and was relieved to read an article by a celebrated young English memoirist who said putting real events in the order they'd happened was a recipe for tedium because life 'is not much of a storyteller'. (His own memoir, which leaps about in time like a *Terminator* movie, is pretty good, but it includes the horrible and premature deaths of his entire family, which gives him an unfair head start in terms of drama and pathos.)

Ditch chronology, though, and you need to find some other organising principle for the incoherent mass of data that accumulates over a lifetime. When pitching the book to my publisher I sketched out a logical chapter outline, with tidy themes and segues and signposts, but as soon as I started writing it was obvious that my roadmap was hopeless: I needed to wander off into the jungle and see where I fetched up. So here I am, in a small clearing, machete in hand, catching my breath and wondering if I'd be better off navigating by the stars.

In the previous chapter, which ends with Dad heading off for Auckland, I skimmed through his first 20 years in a couple of thousand words. But what about the next 20? I'm simultaneously worried that there's not enough to say – the young man gets married, goes into publishing, has kids, smokes too much, carves out a big reputation in the small world of New Zealand letters, loses his mojo, alienates people, gets older, dies – but also far too much: so far I've managed to revisit only a fraction of the letters I photographed in haste in the Katherine Mansfield Reading Room. Two days ago the Hocken Library at Otago University posted me another 350 pages photocopied from their archives of letters between Dad and Charles Brasch from the mid-60s to early 70s. Meanwhile, my sisters and I have found 20 more boxes of Dad's literary stuff – letters, story manuscripts, receipts, Christmas cards, God knows what – stored in our garages and basements and attics. All up, I figure that's about two million words waiting for at least a cursory glance.

I've brought a couple of those boxes up to the bach, including a handful of love letters written by Ernest to Winifred in the 1920s, which my sister Anna brought me a week ago. They seem off-topic for my purposes, yet, last night, right after typing a paragraph that characterised Ernest as a narrow-minded bully, I leafed through these swoony, gentle letters from his youth, addressed to 'My Dear Sweetheart' and 'Dear Breath of Heaven', and noted once again how hopeless it is to try to distil a real person into a few sentences.

Something else, though, has happened since I started writing this.

I was interviewing a writer who'd known Dad. As my final question I asked if they had any gossip, rumours or anecdotes that I might find interesting.

'Well . . .' said the writer.

They paused for quite a while.

'There were matters to do with Robin's private life that were fairly common knowledge, and you don't need to particularly hear *my* version of those. I mean he had affairs, but he wasn't the only person in that era, so it's kind of not interesting. I don't think they were of much importance.'

Actually, hearing for the first time that my father had had affairs and that it was 'fairly common knowledge', seemed thoroughly interesting to me, but the writer had erected a small barrier by saying I didn't need to hear their version and that it was unimportant, and I hadn't prepared myself for a combative kind of interview, so I just said 'Uhuh' and the conversation drifted on to the subject of whether Dad had engaged in the personality feuds that bedevil literary sets (short answer: not often). But the word 'affair' persisted.

A few days later I was at my mother's house, eating supermarket soup at her kitchen table, and I asked her: did Dad have any affairs that she knew of?

Oh yes, said Mum, as if I'd asked her if she'd like a cup of tea. There had been an affair.

Oh.

This felt different from when the writer said it was 'common knowledge'. If Mum said it, it must be true. I felt two things at once: the familiar greedy tingle you get as a journalist when you realise your interviewee has just given you the fact or quote that's going to make your intro; but also a small internal lurch at the idea of my father sleeping with someone other than my mother after they'd married. I didn't feel disgusted or horrified or betrayed or angry, not even surprised, really – affairs happen, and I'd idly wondered about the possibility – but to hear it confirmed still caused a tiny realignment of the planets.

Who was it with, I asked, taking out my phone, turning on the voice recorder and sliding it across the table.

I can't really go into it, she said. You'd put it in the book.

Well, I said, I can't promise that I won't, but I'll show you the chapter before it's published. Go on.

She told me the name. She told me when the affair was (late 1960s), where (Christchurch), how long it went on (not very), how she reacted to it (mostly calmly), and how it had affected the marriage (barely at all, she said). She said the woman had been a friend of theirs, and she had been 'very attractive, very clever, very nice'. I asked if the woman was still alive. I asked Mum if she'd mind if I tracked the woman down. I asked some other impertinent questions about her own sex life and then I had to rinse the soup bowls and get home.

The next day I googled the woman's name, and felt relieved when nothing came up. Then I felt guilty because I knew there were lots of other ways to find people and I wasn't really trying hard enough. Then I felt queasy about the idea of naming the woman when Mum had asked me not to, and about the prospect of chasing down someone in their 70s and asking them about a possible affair of half a century ago. I wondered if my desire to follow this up was just prurience and decided it might well be, but what's the point of a memoir unless you include at least a few warts? And then I thought, Sod it. All this agonising can wait – I've got plenty else to get on with. So many cardboard boxes.

So far, I've written up to the bit where Dad is 20 years old and about to move to Auckland. Mum says the affair happened in his early 30s. That means I have more than a decade to research and write about before I need to summon the courage and cheek to blunder around asking people about sex. In any case, once that's done, once I've learnt all I need to know – it's only then that I'll have to decide how much of it to put into the book.

For now, I'm heading to Auckland, to some time in the late 1950s, when Robin Dudding worked in a biscuit factory and slept in a cemetery. This cowardly decision to delay the inevitable is a huge relief.

7. A freakish notion

On Sunday night (writes newly arrived Aucklander Robin Dudding, aged 20 and a bit, to his mother Winifred in May 1956) he was so broke he went around phone boxes pressing the coin-refund 'Button B' in search of spare pennies, and made a profit of 2d. The next day he pawned his typewriter for £8 and in the evening he had a 'good sleep' on a bench outside the railway station, and woke up to find another bum keeping him company. 'Didn't even get a squeeze out of it amazingly enough. Quite fun – but I don't think I'll do it again.'

He's been working some shifts at the Aulsebrooke's biscuit factory, he says, going half-deaf banging dents out of biscuit tins. He's been down on the docks unloading bananas and beer, chewing gum and fridges. He stole a few bananas, but was too scared of the skits to eat his fill. The other day, he was riding pillion when his mate skidded his motorbike into the back of a taxi ('taxi's fault'), and the next day he was nudged by a slow-moving bus while crossing Customs Street in a dream ('I woke up in time to run away from it'). No big deal. Stop worrying, Mother.

He signs off: 'Please send my dressing gown and Oxford dictionary down – I need them both. R.'

In the two years from January 1956 to late 1957, my father was busy inventing himself, laying the foundations upon which he would build the rest of his life. He was experimenting – with his career, his politics, his friendships, even his name (in Auckland everyone called him 'Bob') – and he seemed aware of the extreme fluidity of the future, of the great weight that might attach to small decisions and chance events. All year, in a stream of letters home, he kept his mother posted.

Auckland is only a springboard – he's saving to be out of the country by next June at the latest. He's seen an interesting job advertised in Taranaki and might apply. He's going to cash in his life insurance and invest in some North Shore land that will double in value once the Harbour Bridge is complete. Then again, he's feeling 'very blue at the present moment – nothing going right' and might move home to Hastings. (None of these things happens.)

He's writing something. 'About September watch for a novel published by RN Dudding.' He's taking some university papers, though he and his lecturer, the poet Allen Curnow, 'had a little tiff, so my chances are getting dimmer & dimmer'. He's just back from a three-week compulsory military training refresher at Hobsonville Air Base, and it rained so heavily they woke in their tents at 4 o'clock in the morning with water lapping around their ears. He's thinking about going back to journalism, even though he had a gutsful of it at the *Herald-Tribune*. He's thinking of auditioning for a play at the Grafton Theatre. He sends his love to Sox the cat.

He's growing a moustache. He's been to see *Blackboard Jungle*, *Rear Window* and *The Dam Busters*, a jazz concert and a Ralph Richardson play, the Henry Moore exhibition that mayor J. H. Luxford has described as 'a nauseating sight', and pianist Benno Moiseiwitsch at the Town Hall. He's got a cold, he's hurt his back and he's got a crook leg. He's so broke he hasn't eaten for three days. His false tooth has fallen out and needs replacing. 'Everybody is having appendicitis – it's about my turn.' He's taking a girl to the Arts Ball (he as a toreador, she as Carmen). He's definitely going to fail his exams, not least because he can't afford the syllabus texts. He's applied for a job at the *Auckland Star*. He's got the job, and the pay's terrible. He's shaved off the moustache.

He's sleeping in various levels of luxury in Penrose, Mt Eden, Remuera, Henderson, Parnell and Milford, and on a railway station bench. He's drinking coffee at the Mocambo; he's stuffing himself for 2 shillings at a chink restaurant; he's had a girl round and made her a lovely salad.

He's almost given up grog apart from a few beers with the other reporters, and he's had no whisky for six months, 'so you will not have to hit a bottle on the head with a shovel again'. He's almost certainly not going to bother sitting his exams – 'I don't feel like pandering to the examiners'. He's reviewing theatre and writing about rugby league for the *Star*. He's moonlighting as editor of the *Parnell Post*, a local freebie that runs front-page exposés about unsanitary public toilets and unreliable buses. He's got hay-fever.

He's bought some new clothes – the coat is red and purple, the trousers white and grey and the shoes light tan. 'I am the best dressed man in the office if not in town now.'

'PS: Passed Eng.'

What I like most about this lovely, funny time capsule from the middle of the 20th century is that it shows my father trying on new voices as well as new clothes. With the unpredictable squeak/roar of an adolescent boy whose voice is breaking, his letters lurch between a doting son's fond chit-chat and the ironic nihilism of a hard-boiled noir detective. It's hard to tell whether he's trying to shock his mother or make her laugh, though probably both.

Of sleeping at the railway station, he writes:

> Now I know as well as you do that sleeping on park benches is not a very wise or desirable thing to do but in the circumstances it was just the only thing to do. And it was all good experience. I can't write about bums and depression days in N.Z. unless I sleep on a park bench at least once. And as you know or mightn't know, depression days are the only things New Zealanders write about. That's not my fault.
>
> The point is – if I'm going to write at all I prefer to write honestly more or less. I needn't have told you that I slept on a park bench or my room was damp and my landlady was a drunkard or that I had an accident on a motor-bike or I worked as a wharfie or if in the future I assault a cop and spend a week in Mt Eden or get married to a slut or break my neck on a banana skin, or anything else. But as a reporter more or less I see that as all news [. . .]
>
> Your upbringing has left me with a certain amount of honesty anyhow even if it isn't directed in altogether the right directions [but] you'll never stop worrying anyhow – so what's the use.
>
> That's life isn't it. And that is what we are all here for – to live. So what's the odds.

Only occasionally does he address his father directly, and his tone is sour by comparison.

> I sleep on a park bench and get soaking wet and don't get even a sniffle. Not a sniffle after sleeping in mud in camp and in a wet room in Wynyard Street and walking to work in the rain because I couldn't afford the bus fare.
>
> Then lo and behold I get a job that I have to think in. A job that is worrying me because I don't think I'm good enough. At the same time I move in to a warm, dry room with a soft, dry bed and a return to three good meals a day. And lo and behold I get the Flu'. [. . .] I think that is extra significant on top of the fact that they reckon all colds are a psychological phenomenon.
>
> Another sign of gutlessness I guess. I should be able to recognise it, after you, Pa, have beaten the fact of that unusual weakness into me since I was knee high to a grasshopper.

Given the letter's unrelenting ironic tone, I've no idea if he's kicking his father's shins for the fun of it, or expressing genuine angst. Again, probably both. I suspect there's also a covert 'fuck you' to his National-voting Dad in a December 1956 letter where he mentions, apropos of nothing much, that 'it's pounds to peanuts that the security police have got me tabbed as a subversive character with communistic tendencies because of my associates'. During the nationwide 1951 waterfront dispute, Ernest the baker had happily undermined the locked-out unionists by unloading his own flour at Napier Wharf with Robin's help, something Robin kept very quiet once he was in Auckland and learnt the meaning of the word 'scab'. Ernest can't have been happy at the thought of his son fraternising with the wrong crowd.

Even if this talk of security police is a wind-up, it isn't an entirely paranoid notion. 1956 was the year the Security Intelligence Service was founded, mainly to sniff out Soviet sympathisers in the wake of Australia's thrilling Petrov Affair of 1954, when a Russian diplomat defected. New Zealand authorities admitted (but only in 2009) that they had spied on the writer, feminist and one-time communist Elsie Locke, who was corresponding with Dad by the early 1960s if not earlier. Poet Hone Tuwhare, whom Dad would first publish in 1960, was also a member of the Communist Party until the Soviet invasion of Hungary. Frank Sargeson had once been in the Young Communist League – maybe the spooks were snooping on him and his Takapuna shack.

Dad was overstating the case, though. In early 2015 I received a polite letter from the head of the Security Intelligence Service to say she could find no trace of Robin Dudding in their files. 'It would appear neither your father, nor the magazines he edited, was ever considered to be of security significance.' I can't help finding this a bit disappointing.

There's another story in this 23-letter sequence spanning two years – a three-act romantic comedy in glimpses. Robin makes passing, mildly strutting reference to various women, but one figure stands out. First she's 'a girl who goes to the same lectures as me'. Later, she's 'a passing girl-friend named Lois Miller' whom he's taken to a reporter's social and invited home for that lovely salad. Next though, he writes that Lois has 'gone home to her regular boy', and 'I've lost interest there'.

I know how this ends, but that doesn't reduce the suspense of turning to the next letter, looking for evidence of the rom-com's final act.

At the *Auckland Star* Dad chased at least one hard-news story. He told his mother he was on the trail of a 'tough crowd' of drug-dealers selling to kids, 'but for God's sake don't repeat that in any form or I will find myself coshed'. He wasn't sure if he would be able to get the full story and hoped 'I don't have to dope myself to get to them'.

In a scrapbook of Dad's *Star* clippings I can't find any big scoop about a drugs ring, so I guess he never did crack that case wide open. He did, however, file reports on milk production in Northland and the future of the crockery industry. He wrote rugby league match reports for the sports desk. And as in Hastings he found himself drawn towards the *Star*'s arts desk (or Queers' Corner, as the rest of the typewriter-bashing, chain-smoking journos called it). He reviewed as many plays and concerts and exhibitions as he could get away with, but the most exciting cultural activity was happening somewhere else entirely.

He found the door to Auckland's literary scene down on the docks, while working as a 'seagull' soon after he arrived. Each day at 8am, crowds of men – itinerants, immigrants, university students, underemployed labourers – would congregate at the 'bureau', a shed on a wharf at the bottom of Queen Street, where they'd put their name down for a day's work, then wait to be called. The seagulls supplemented the wharf's union labour, or handled cargoes so noxious the wharfies wouldn't touch them: lugging bulk phosphate or sulphur was the closest thing to a day in hell.

While you waited for your name to be called you'd sit around yakking, and if there was no work at all you'd head to the pub, or to the Parnell Baths a mile and a half along the waterfront.

The best result, though, was if you got signed up by the bureau clerk just before a heavy downpour, in which case you'd have to stop work and play cards on full pay. The new kid told his mother he'd never seen so many different nationalities together at the same time.

> In our game of cards there were 8 playing and they included a Dutchy, a pole, a Samoan, a pom, a Maori, another Maori and I think two New Zealanders – me and another bloke. No only me the other I remember was a red-blooded Irishman. You could hardly understand what was going on.

He especially hit it off with a young English-born artist, Anthony Stones, known as Tony, who'd emigrated to New Zealand as a teenager four years earlier. On a day when the work was thin, Tony led Robin back up Queen Street and they turned left into Vulcan Lane then left again through the door of the Queen's Ferry. This was the unofficial headquarters of Auckland's literary set, and there Robin discovered a society of people who talked in ways he'd not heard before. He stayed, and listened, and eventually started to talk a little himself.

In 1988, Dad was asked by *Metro* magazine to write a piece remembering a favourite Auckland place. He wrote it, even though in his covering note he invited the editor to file it in her wastepaper basket: 'I had always sworn not to indulge in autobiography, and this turns out to be a précised bit of just that: who could possibly be interested.'

Rather than one place he named dozens, drifting sideways into a sketch of his 1950s social and literary life – 'a potpourri with its associated risk of a slop-bucket of dropped names'.

It's a warm, elegant piece, yet typically of what little he wrote for a public audience, its language is so efficient, the facts so neatly packed and any sentimentality so controlled, that to me it's not half as fun as the gawky, squawking letters he fired off to his mum. He also straightened out some embarrassing kinks: there's no reference to 'chink' restaurants, no lists of ethnicities where a Māori is seen as someone other than a New Zealander.

The Queen's Ferry, he wrote, was:

> Haunt of Kevin Ireland, Tony Stones, John Graham, Don Terris, Mike Illingworth, Peter Milligan, Keith Patterson, Moss Gee, Dave Walsh, Rod (Machiavelli) Smith, Ted and Ian Middleton, Dick Scott, Bill Moller, Frank Knipe, Uncle Tom Cobley and all . . . and eventually Crump, out of the bush and soon determined to show that while the rest of us just talked about it, he *would* write. And did.

To that list I'll add Maurice Shadbolt, Maurice Duggan, John Yelash, A. R. D. Fairburn, Nigel Cook . . . Clearly this was a man's world, though it doesn't help that women were barred from the Ferry's public bar – they were allowed in the upstairs room only.

This loose association of artists, authors, poets, playwrights, students, political thinkers, publishers, academics, historians and bullshit artists had other stomping grounds too: the Occidental next door; the Globe round the corner where you might have found the legendary printer Bob Lowry; the milk bars and tearooms of Queen Street; the handful of restaurants that comprised the city's embryonic dining scene.

There were literary outposts beyond the city centre. At

Esmonde Road, Takapuna – still a mangrove-swamp dead-end rather than an on-ramp to the Harbour Bridge motorway – Frank Sargeson, an elder statesman of NZ Lit at 53 or so, held court behind his famous hedge. Sargeson's visitors included Kay and Karl Stead. The army hut in his garden had only recently been vacated by Janet Frame, who had written her first novel *Owls Do Cry* there before leaving for Europe.

Nearby in Birkenhead, playwright and author John Graham hatched a mad scheme to get rich growing a vast crop of 'Moneymaker' tomatoes on 13 heavily mortgaged acres of market garden. The plan was to spend the profits on converting a packing shed into a theatre, where Graham and Sargeson and others would then produce their plays. At weekends the now-tight trio of Robin Dudding and Tony Stones and Kevin Ireland, and perhaps some others from the Queen's Ferry gang, took the ferry to the Shore to slave at the vines alongside Sargeson and John Graham, as well as John's wife Betty and their children.

'It's more or less a literary community led by Frank Sargeson where we work in the garden all day and talk all night,' Robin informed his mother, but she didn't know the half of it. The weekend volunteers subsisted on cups of tea, toast topped with sliced tomato and grated cheese, and half-gallon containers of real, unfortified wine from Maté Brajkovich's Kumeu vineyards – a rare treat in an era when the average New Zealander drank 80 litres of beer a year and only a litre-and-a-half of wine.

In the *Metro* piece Dad describes 'red wine soaked hours pruning, picking, polishing and packing', and invites the reader to picture:

> Frank washing off the kauri clay-dust at end of day while practising his *Joy of the Worm*-type handstands in the sea. Ireland, dancing bollocky among the tomato plants at midday to the roar of Beethoven's Ninth from the open window. Or, midnight 40-gallon drum music from the hayshed to keep the neighbours (quite distant) alert.

In February 1957 Dad wrote home instructing his parents to withdraw '500 smackers' from his insurance policy so he could invest it in the market garden for 12 months. In her first reply his mother asked what a 'smacker' was, and in her next she said the policy wasn't worth a tenth of that. So Robin didn't invest, which was just as well – a month later an unseasonal heavy frost destroyed the entire crop. The mortgage folded. John Graham was bankrupted. Dad bought John's 1930 Pontiac for £35 at the auction then returned it 'to its rightful owner after a hair-raising ride or two'.

Then there were the parties – especially the ones at Jocelyn and Odo Strewe's in Titirangi, or at Irene and Bob Lowry's at One Tree Hill. It was heady pleasure, Dad recalls in *Metro*:

> for someone from silent Hawke's Bay to eavesdrop. All this talk, endless talk – even if it was only as basic as some admired poet putting the hard word on some beauteous female, with lots of Yeatsian and Dylan Thomas quotes thrown in for good measure.

(In an earlier draft he's less discreet. Instead of 'some admired poet', it reads 'Allen Curnow'.)

One day, after one of the Lowry parties, something

important happened. This is a story Kevin Ireland has told before, even turned into a poem, and I'd thought it had a suspiciously burnished feel – too tidy, too cute. But as he tells it again in the sitting room of his home in Devonport, the North Shore suburb where he's a local celebrity complete with OBE and a huge portrait in the public library, he swears it's the unvarnished truth.

After leaving the party the two of them stumbled back to Robin's current digs – a twin-bed bach in a Parnell back garden. They had drunk way too much – each had a spew on the way home. They crawled into their cots and the next morning they lay there self-pityingly, occasionally groaning into consciousness. Eventually Robin made a cup of tea, which they managed to keep down. They each sucked back a roll-your-own and got talking the kind of talk you can have only when you're properly hungover.

Robin was in a black depression. 'It's all right for you, Kev,' he said. 'You know you're going to write poetry all your life and that's it.'

Robin *wanted* to write but he had nothing to write about; it was just a vague ambition without any proper focus. And what he had already written he didn't like. (Kevin had seen some of Robin's scribblings, short stories and so on, 'and though mine were terrible his were worse, and he was very self-critical'.)

'Anyway,' Kevin tells me, 'I said to him – and it was inspired, one of the few moments of inspiration I've ever suffered from as far as friends are concerned – I said, "You know, Charlie Brasch can't keep going on forever. We all need a bloody editor. That's one of the most marvellous and vital literary jobs there is. A good editor is one of the hardest things to find in literature. Why don't you do that?" And he said, "Jesus, that's a bloody good idea."

'That's,' says Kevin in capital letters, 'How. It. Went! From that time on, I'd sowed it in Bob's mind.

'Bob had a couple of bottles of beer, and after we'd had a little bit of toast and another cigarette we opened the beer and we drank to success. We did all the right things, and the gods looked on it with great favour because we followed the ritual. All the protocols were boxed and ticked.'

Or, as Kevin put it in the poem he wrote after Dad died: 'At twenty you have no idea of how / a freakish notion can freeze / on the wind and shape you forever.'

Not long after that, Kevin and a couple of friends (not including Dad) put together a little magazine called *Mate* and paid Bob Lowry £20 to print it. It looked good but Kevin couldn't carry it on – he was itching to travel.

Before he left, Kevin approached Robin. '"Y'know, everyone thinks this is another one-issue magazine, but I reckon there's a second issue in it – would you like to do it?" And Bob did. And it was so much better than the first one.'

Dad's first-ever literary magazine, *Mate* 2, published in November 1958, was co-edited with David Walsh, but from issue 3 he ran the show, with Tony Stones as 'assistant editor'. The cover illustration by Tony harks back to his and Robin's seagulling days – it's a line drawing of George, a Māori chap who, while waiting for the bureau clerk to call out his name, would sit on a bollard, pull out his chess set and take anyone on.

Here's the contributor list on the contents page of *Mate* 2:

Odo Strewe
Peter Fairbrother
Maurice Gee
Alan Roddick
Lois Miller
Barry Crump
Gordon Challis
Frank Sargeson
Kevin Ireland
John Graham
Charles Doyle

Barry Crump's story was his first published work: a rollicking yarn about hard-case deer-hunters called 'A Good Keen Man' that would later grow into a book that sold in astounding quantities, turning Crump into a celebrity and earning him a genuine fortune, something the Queen's Ferry set would watch with admiration and envy.

The solitary female name on the list is familiar too, of course.

Sometime in 1956, in an Auckland coffee shop, Jean Watson (a university student, an unpublished writer and one of the many future partners of Barry Crump) introduced her friend Robin Dudding to a girl she knew: Lois Miller. It turned out that Robin and Lois were taking some of the same English papers, though she usually sat at the back and he near the front – she'd spotted him up there in his military training uniform. Funnily enough they shared birthdays – 7 December – though Lois was one year older.

Robin was intrigued by this very self-possessed woman

with big eyes and strong cheekbones, who reminded him a little of *Casablanca*-era Ingrid Bergman. The skinny boy from Hawke's Bay made no particular impression on Lois. He was interesting enough to talk to, but then quite a lot of blokes were. She had plenty of boyfriends.

They ran into each other a bit and went to a few things together, but Lois was rather more interested in Robin's best mate Tony Stones. In fact Lois and Tony were an item for a while, until Tony dropped her in favour of a dramatic woman named Cushla, who already had a couple of children. And later Lois took up with a slightly older man – a painter on the fringes of the Queen's Ferry crowd whom she already knew from her hometown of Cambridge in the Waikato. She returned with him to Cambridge in late 1956 and they got engaged.

If this was *Back to the Future*, this is the part where my sisters and I start turning semi-transparent in the family photo.

In Cambridge, Lois was technically living with her parents, but as the engagement stretched into months, and then a year, the overnight stays with her fiancé were becoming an affront to small-town sensibilities. I've heard divergent accounts of what happened next.

According to Kevin Ireland, Robin – and just about everyone else in the overwhelmingly male circles they moved in – took close note of Lois from the moment she walked into the café that day with Jean Watson. But when sifting through her suitors Lois made a dreadful choice. Her Cambridge fellow was a 'total poser', someone who was glamorous but 'impotent in every sense of the word', 'an appalling person', 'an absolute phony', and so on. Kevin's splenetic loyalty to his temporarily-passed-over friend, 60 years after the fact, is fearsome to behold.

Anyway, says Kevin, once Lois discovered the guy was useless she was much chastened, so now she was looking for the real thing. Robin moved in like Speedy Gonzales – there was a flash of light and there was Robin. To be more specific, when Robin got hold of Lois's number and rang her in Cambridge, she told him she was done with the phony and wanted out.

'That was the moment Bob had been waiting for, because he was desperately in love with her,' says Kevin, in his rumbling, half-chuckling, professional yarn-spinning voice. 'Bob was the knight on a white charger, and he went racing down and collected her and whisked her up to Auckland and the next thing is they're married.'

Nice story, says Mum when I talk to her later that week, but largely untrue.

For a start, the fiancé was an excellent artist – definitely not a phony. Yes, she did call off the engagement (for reasons she tells me only after extracting a firm promise I really won't put it in the book), but there was no 'Rescue me' phone conversation with Robin. There was no mercy dash from Auckland by a knight on a white charger.

In that case, I ask her, what *did* happen? I'd like to understand the sequence of events, but I'm also keen to know what made her realise that she *was* interested, after all, in the thin-faced, quiet young man I've seen in the photos, with his crooked teeth and a crooked smile that could easily be mistaken for a smirk, with his heavily Brylcreemed side-parted dark hair and his perpetual cigarette. Can she describe her and Dad's sudden lurch from friends to affianced lovers?

My mother is an unusually difficult interview subject. Even when she isn't evading a question, the neurological scrambling from her stroke can turn any conversation into a semantic adventure. She knows what's going on and at times can speak utterly fluently. But sometimes you need to find a comfortable position as she haltingly constructs a sentence in which some, perhaps all, of the words have been replaced with surreal alternates. You then repeat back a paraphrase of what you presume she meant, and she confirms or denies or, worse still, attempts to clarify, in which case you're down a whole new rabbit hole.

What happened? I ask. How did he win you over?

'Well,' says Mum. 'He was keen I suppose. Yeah.'

Yes of course. But what *happened*? I presume you were keen too?

'Well, no.'

(I briefly wonder if by 'no' she actually means 'yes', but dismiss the possibility. She seldom mixes those two up.)

Look, I say. A minute ago you said you had loads of boyfriends, so you obviously weren't so short of options that you had to accept Robin by default, were you?

'No. But I thought he would make a good father.'

Ah! This is progress. But – is that enough on its own to decide to marry? This is courtship in the era of beat poetry, early rock 'n' roll and Oswald Mazengarb's scandalised inquiry into teen promiscuity in New Zealand. She must have found other things about Robin appealing as well.

Did you like his twinkling eyes? I ask. Or his deep voice? His bony feet? His thrusting manhood?

'Oh, all of those things,' says Mum, and she cackles for a while without giving any more detail.

I explain that understanding your parents' courtship is an important existential matter for any child. It's the historical moment where one's future is on a knife edge, vulnerable to the outcome of a particular conversation, a well-timed offer of a cup of coffee, a pheromonal zephyr.

Mum identifies this as horseshit, and laughs at me.

I point out that we've been bickering for 45 minutes and in that time she's not even answered the first of what I'd hoped would be 20 or so questions that would take us into the late 1960s, and we're still only up to 1957, and she cackles even louder.

Eventually I get a little closer to the truth. A few weeks after my failed interrogation of Mum I find a letter from Robin to his mother.

He's writing from Cambridge. The letter's handwritten and undated, but it must be around September 1957. He's taken a fortnight's hitch-hiking holiday from the *Auckland Star* with the intention of visiting Rotoiti, Whakatāne, Mt Maunganui, Wellington, Hastings, Taranaki – heck, maybe Ninety Mile Beach. However, 'six days later and I haven't got past Cambridge having called in to see Lois for 1/2 an hour. I am staying with her parents . . .'

He continues the letter a couple of days later. He's finally dragged himself away from the Millers' place, but the rest of the grand tour has been truncated to a brief visit to Whakatāne, and he's going to Cambridge once more before hitching back to Auckland.

Surely this is the mercy dash by Dad that Kevin was describing, even if he was hitching rather than riding a white charger, and even if Lois didn't actually follow him back to Auckland for a few more months. Something happened between the two of them in Cambridge. He hasn't actually proposed yet but the sign-off to his letter suggests marriage is on his mind, even if it's disguised as daft leg-pulling.

> Sorry this is so short and sweet but there just really isn't anything to tell you except that I'm getting married in the first week of February, that I've joined the Roman Catholic Church and that I've got a charge of manslaughter against me.
>
> Love Robin
>
> P.S: My wife to be is a Maori–Japanese cross and she is 47 years of age.

To be precise, his wife-to-be is a 22-year-old Pākehā woman. By February 1958 she's back in Auckland and he has properly proposed. In early March he hires a small car in Auckland, and he and Lois, and their friends Cushla and Tony Stones who married just a week earlier, squeeze in for the drive to Hastings, where there'll be a wedding on the 8th. Robin is at the wheel as they hurtle down the spine of the North Island, and every so often he yells, at the top of his voice: 'Isn't it marvellous to be young and alive in the middle of the 20th century!'

8. Men of Achievement 1974

LATE 1997. Comet Hale-Bopp's Earth flyby has come and gone. President Clinton has been having sexual relations with that woman Monica Lewinsky but no one else knows about it yet. Mike Tyson has bitten a piece of Evander Holyfield's ear off, and a Scottish woman has published her first book about a boy wizard. Ellen DeGeneres has declared herself a lesbian, there's a new film out about the *Titanic* and James Bond is played by Pierce Brosnan. Princess Diana is recently dead. So is Mother Teresa.

In New Zealand a former schoolteacher called Jenny Shipley is about to overthrow her colleague Jim Bolger to become New Zealand's first woman prime minister. A striking singer-songwriter called Bic Runga has released her debut album *Drive*, and the fiction winner at the national book awards is Alan Duff's sequel to *Once Were Warriors*. In Auckland a 328m-tall observation tower has just had its official opening, and the city's mayor is a homophobic gym owner called Les Mills.

Robin Dudding, 61, of Torbay, hasn't edited a literary magazine of his own for quite a while. After a late-career return to the queasy comforts of a fulltime job as a sub-editor for the *Listener* he's recently retired, mainly because his cigarette-poisoned lungs have left him so short of breath and energy that getting up and down the stairs at the *Listener* offices in Dominion Road was getting too hard. He hasn't smoked a cigarette for years now, but he still misses the taste. One of his hips is buggered too, though he's on a waiting list for a replacement early in the new year.

And me? I'm living in Newcastle in the north of England, and wishing I wasn't.

In my 27 years I'd learnt to walk and talk and read and count, I'd finished school, done a science degree, been flatting, played in some bands, learnt how to drink and smoke a joint, toured New Zealand for six weeks as the pianist for a monstrous drag queen called Diamond Lil, and done a few shifts proofreading television listings for the *Listener*.

I'd shouldered a blue Macpac backpack and travelled on self-defeatingly tiny budgets around Europe and the Middle East, eating boiled rice and sleeping in parks. In London I pulled pints and temped in an office where I spent six months drawing computer diagrams of the railway line between Tilbury and Southend-on-Sea before an engineer changed the route and everything I'd drawn was discarded. In Cambridge I frothed cappuccinos and failed to sell double-glazing over the phone. I swabbed the decks on an Egyptian dive boat and busked with a tambourine and a guitar-strumming friend in front of the unfortunate customers of Barcelona's street cafés. I spent three years, in other words, being one of those mid-20s antipodean moochers on their OE who feels like they're vaguely counter-cultural and forging their own unique history, but is actually selecting from a standardised menu of procrastinatory options.

Despite an idiot shyness that kept me virgin much older than seemed reasonable I had a few girlfriends, before chancing upon an especially nice one at a party in Finsbury Park, north London, and hitching my fate to hers. She was Scottish. It had been a couple of years since I persuaded her to come and live with me in New Zealand, but after the sudden death of her father a year ago, we were back in England to be near to her mum for a bit.

So. Back in miserable England with its squatting grey skies and stupid front-loading washing machines and annoying banks and morose shop assistants and squashed-together houses. Back in wonderful England with its amazing newspapers and unabashedly intelligent TV presenters, its smooth domesticated countryside in a range of bright deciduous greens that I found myself traitorously preferring to New Zealand's darker primeval shades. England, with all those streets and placenames that immediately felt like home even if I only knew them from the Monopoly board or *Sherlock Holmes*. England, with its accents and cynicism and class hatred and post-colonial malaise and ceaseless drinking and clever conversation, and its clever writers – the ones I met aged five as well as the ones I'd only recently found: Richmal Crompton, Enid Blyton and whoever wrote *Rupert the Bear*; Christianna Brand, E. Nesbit and E. L. Travers (even if she was really Australian); J. R. R. Tolkien and C. S. Lewis, Richard Adams and Joan Aiken, Alan Garner and Roald Dahl; the old fascist H. G. Wells (from a compendium of his sci-fi that

Dad gave me when I was 10, which I ploughed through only quarter-enjoying); P. G. Wodehouse and Agatha Christie and Kenneth Grahame; Orwell and his fustier fellow writing-style advisers Fowler and Gower; Amis the Younger, Julian Barnes and Ian McEwan; Jeanette Winterson, A. S. Byatt and Kazuo Ishiguro.

I loved and hated the place, and though I was happy enough to be there when it was just a base for adventures, I'd not planned to be back again this soon.

We were in Newcastle because that's the nearest city to my mother-in-law's dot-on-the-map village in the Scottish borders. Newcastle, I decided swiftly, was the worst place in the world. Whenever I got in a cab the driver would notice an accent and ask where I was from, and when I said New Zealand he'd look at me in horror and confusion and ask why I was here when I could be there. One driver seemed near tears as he told me how just a year earlier he'd tried to migrate to New Zealand and had all the papers in order and the flights booked but then his wife got cold feet at the last minute.

To minimise homesickness, I wanted to live near the sea. We found a cheap, grotty place in Whitley Bay, a faded resort on the North Sea coast that fell out of fashion once tourists realised the sea in Spain was 10 degrees warmer and the beer cheaper. Now it was home to the near-derelict Spanish City funfair that Mark Knopfler once sang about, as well as all-hours nightclubs, sticky-floored pubs selling dangerously cheap spirits, and the occasional baby seal that came ashore from the frigid ocean to rest on the sand, freaking out our Labrador, Judy, who possibly saw a family resemblance in the sleek head and long whiskers.

We were told that the week before we moved into our unheatably cold flat above a wedding-dress shop, someone was stabbed a few yards from our door while queueing to get into a club. But generally the crowds milling in the street every evening – women in Geordie night-time uniform of microskirt, boob tube and no coat despite the snow flurries; men in regulation chinos and bright shirt – are extraordinarily friendly, even (in fact especially) the women crouching in doorways for a piss, the men slumped half-conscious against fences, and the occasional couple down on the sand fucking against the old stone seawall.

I needed a job, so I sent my suspiciously patchy CV to every organisation in a 50-mile radius that might need someone good with a semicolon and a split infinitive. The only interview I got was with the *Shields Gazette*, an evening tabloid that for 30 pence or so provided its community of unemployed former miners and shipbuilders with a parochial yet gamely sensationalist news agenda; shortly after I started there as a sub-editor the screaming front-page lead was an interview with a South Shields man whose rubbish bins had been knocked over and who was incensed because the council refused to come round and set them upright again. In the photo accompanying the story the man looked very angry.

When I left home at 6 o'clock it was still three hours till sunrise. I would shuffle through slushy snow, catch a train, shuffle through more slush, take a ferry south across the Tyne and descend below street level into a bunker of an office. By the time I re-emerged at 3 o'clock and headed for the ferry home the sun would be down already.

I got to know a few of the ferry regulars.

'New Zealand!' marvelled a short, bearded, middle-aged

man who worked for the council. He told me he planned to move there one day, where he would retrain and work as a midwife. I nodded encouragingly.

The happiest moment of my three months at the *Gazette* was the day my colleague Noreen shoved me in the ribs and showed me the headline she'd just written for a story about a minor house fire caused by a towel left on a heater. The headline had to be squeezed a little to fit the space, but it was still perfect: 'Towelling inferno.'

I laughed and laughed and found it difficult to stop.

Just before I left for a job at a regional Sunday tabloid based in central Newcastle, the travel editor handed me a freebie – a weekend in Mayrhofen, Austria, including some skiing lessons, free Glühwein and a visit to the village hermit, an old bearded man who lived in a tiny hut halfway up a mountain, where he distilled his own rocket-fuel schnapps.

As my train hissed to a halt in a chocolate-box village tucked between snowy Tyrolean mountains I figured life was looking up, but by evening I thought I was getting a cold and by the next morning I had a blinding headache and noticed my back was coming up in watery blisters that popped when I reached round to touch them. The internet was still rudimentary, and I barely knew any German, and I was embarrassed, so I made an expensive phonebox call to Newcastle for medical advice. My wife checked my symptoms in our *Pears Cyclopaedia* and told me I had either syphilis or chicken pox.

I survived both the chicken pox and the skiing lessons, relying on nips of Glühwein and the hermit's moonshine to mask my heavy-boned fever, then limped back to England trying not to scratch the blisters that now covered my entire body.

I survived my year in Newcastle too, relying on pints of Stella Artois and bottles of Newcastle Brown Ale to mask my desperate urge to be anywhere else – much the same method that seemed to keep the locals going.

My new job was still pretty terrible but also perversely enjoyable. Like most I've encountered, the subs' desk at the *Sunday Sun* was a collection of highly articulate, near-alcoholic misfits unleashing their perfectionism on something they knew would still be shit even once all the spelling mistakes were fixed. We raged against the insanity of the editor, the ignorance of the reporters and the stupidity of the readers, and spent the lulls between deadlines in near-hysterical efforts to antagonise and amuse each other. I almost managed to get the headline 'Clogs popped' above a story about an especially tragic suicide in the Netherlands, before the chief sub-editor vetoed it. Near the end of each week we wrote fake letters to the editor, because we never got any from real readers. At lunchtime we drank.

At home the music from the club next door shook the walls, and the music from the pair of would-be club DJs who moved in upstairs and practised their craft daily shook the ceiling. One day our stupid front-loading washing machine flooded, destroying the ceiling of the wedding-dress shop below us, as well as a number of expensive dresses.

Eventually we moved to London, where I would, mercifully, find more rewarding employment, but in early 1998 we went back to Newcastle for the weekend for a wedding.

The night before the wedding, I was at a friend of a friend's place drinking a pre-pub beer. There was a small TV in the corner tuned to BBC Two, and Richard Herring and Stewart

Lee's mildly surreal comedy sketch show *This Morning with Richard Not Judy* was playing. My back was to the screen, but then I heard a familiar string of syllables: 'Robin Nelson Dudding'.

For a second I assumed I'd imagined it, that it was the auditory version of the patriotic reflex all New Zealanders abroad know, where you spot a 'Z' somewhere in a page of text and your eye leaps to it in expectation of the '-ealand' that must follow but usually doesn't.

But no. I'd heard it right. I turned to see the camera zooming in on a black-and-white headshot of a scowling face encircled by dark hair. It was Dad – in his full early-70s glory: crooked self-cut fringe, shaggy shoulder-length bob merging into a full Karl Marx beard, a glimpse of lower lip below the overhanging moustache.

The camera shakily settled on the photo and its surrounding text, and a portentous voice-over continued: 'Robin is an editor from Hastings in New Zealand and is married to Lois Yvonne Miller. They have one son and five daughters. If you are interested in knowing more about Robin Nelson Dudding, he is also listed in *Who's Who in New Zealand*.'

The camera pulled back out as the book was closed, revealing a red cover with a gold embossed title, which the voice read out: 'MEN OF ACHIEVEMENT 1974'.

Well, this was thoroughly weird.

I pointed, incredulous, at the screen, and turned to my friend – 'Did you see that? That was my dad!' – but by the time I got his attention the picture had already cross-faded back to Herring and Lee on the sofas of their faux breakfast TV set, cheerfully complaining that no one ever seemed to find the 'Men of Achievement 1974' segment funny.

Which was an explanation of sorts. It seemed that during every episode they would pluck out some unfortunate 'man of achievement' and his silly 1970s mugshot from this pointless old book, for a few moments of deadpan mockery.

It was strangely unsettling to stumble across this artefact of Dad's existence so far from home and so out of context. I rang Dad as soon as time zones allowed to let him know that the BBC had taken the time to take the piss out of him on British national TV. He said he had a hazy memory of receiving a letter inviting him to be in some sort of international directory, where you paid nothing but had the opportunity to buy a ridiculously overpriced edition in embossed goatskin or some such. He'd sent the form off, but didn't waste his money buying a copy.

He emailed me a few days later: 'Ask those smart asses from BbC if they can produce 5 fillies and 1 colt, tell em it is harder than looks, especially with a beard.'

It was funny, sure, but I also felt slightly sad about this TV cameo, because 'man of achievement' wasn't how I thought of Dad these days. When I was little I knew he was terribly important in some way, but by my teens I'd noticed this didn't translate into anyone I met ever having heard of him.

Now, in my 20s, I knew he was remembered and presumably respected in the small world of NZ Lit, and I still got a little frisson when I read the arts pages of a New Zealand publication and spotted a name that I remembered meeting as a kid, or proofreading a story of, or playing ping-pong doubles with, but it all seemed such a long time ago. His magazine *Islands* had fizzled and died a decade before. Subbing at the *Listener* was a respectable job, but I suspected he got more satisfaction from the lunchtime table-tennis than the work itself. And now he seemed old and disappointed and worn-out – literally, in the case of the arthritic hip that was finally replaced over the New Zealand summer. I wasn't even sure he was especially proud of the things he'd achieved back in the days when he had a bit more life in him.

I was wrong, of course. He wasn't quite finished. And he *was* proud, though he liked to give the impression that he wasn't. And he did matter. It's just that it would be a couple of decades before I bothered finding out enough about him to rediscover that fact.

9. A different star

As well as friends and family, I interview some of the people Dad worked with – poets and authors, editors and publishers, academics and critics. I'm mostly looking for funny stories, or important events I haven't already encountered in his correspondence, or adult perspectives on events I half-remember from my childhood. But while the recorder's running, and after they've confirmed Dad had an extraordinary beard and liked talking about chickens and had seemed rather dour in the 1980s, it would be odd not to seek their professional opinion on something else. Namely, what did they make of Robin Dudding the editor? Were those magazines of his really that big a deal? Was he any good? Was he, in short, a Man of Achievement or not?

There are good reasons to treat their answers with caution. Most of them, at one time or another, had their work published by Dad, so it stands to reason that they would endorse his excellent judgement. Most of them were also, to some extent or another, personal friends as well as colleagues or collaborators. They may also have felt bound by politeness, when talking to the son, to refrain from revealing that the father was actually a misguided fool of no account. Also, apart from a small number of well-known feuds and spats (most of them involving the reliably disputatious writer and academic C. K. Stead) it sometimes feels like there's an omertà within NZ Lit that keeps anyone from bagging anyone else in public – admitting, say, that you find Writer X's famous book unreadably dull, or that you think Poet Y has built a career on sentimental doggerel, or that the only genuine talent Author Z has demonstrated is in writing applications for the succession of government funding grants they keep getting to write books no one reads. (Naturally, in private and with no recorders running, these conversations proceed merrily.)

Yet for all those caveats, it is striking how everyone I interview reaches for superlatives. Editor Dudding was, I am told, 'the best editor we've ever had'; the 'father of a generation' and someone of 'immense' influence. He was a 'lighthouse', a 'cult figure', a 'guru' and a 'cultural hero'.

To recap: what he's remembered for is his editorship of three literary magazines: *Mate* in the 1950s and 60s, *Landfall* in the 60s and 70s, then *Islands* in the 70s and 80s.

He was the first publisher of many writers who went on to be a big deal, including Barry Crump. Others he spotted first, or at least early, included Maurice Gee, Peter Bland, Kevin Ireland, Witi Ihimaera, Keri Hulme, Patricia Grace, Bill Manhire, Ian Wedde, Alan Brunton, Sam Hunt, Bob Orr, Yvonne Du Fresne, Albert Wendt, Margaret Sutherland, Fiona Kidman, Greg McGee, Anne Kennedy, Jenny Bornholdt and Elizabeth Nannestad.

He published C.K. Stead and Vincent O'Sullivan and

Maurice Shadbolt; Fleur Adcock and Elsie Locke and Marilyn Duckworth. He was always looking for the new thing, but they'd generally share covers with writers who'd already made their name – Frank Sargeson and Kendrick Smithyman, Hone Tuwhare and Janet Frame, James K. Baxter and Louis Johnson, Bill Pearson and Maurice Duggan.

Visual art was always part of the mix. Artists who designed a cover or illustrated a story included Ralph Hotere, Doris Lusk, Michael Smither, Toss Woollaston, Michael Illingworth, Pat Hanly, Colin McCahon, Gordon Walters, Tony Fomison, Don Binney, Garth Tapper, Philip Trusttum, Jeffrey Harris, Brent Wong, Nigel Brown, Peter Siddell, Dick Frizzell, Barry Lett, Gregory O'Brien, Joanna Paul and photographer Marti Friedlander. In *Islands* 10 he went art-crazy and reproduced works by 19 people, each accompanied by 300 words from the artist explaining why this was their favourite work.

He published 71 magazines in all plus a handful of standalone books: a comic novel by Barry Mitcalfe, several poetry volumes and a collection of autobiographical essays called *Beginnings*. As a freelance editor for other publishers he had a hand in many dozens more.

That's a solid CV. But lots of people publish stuff, and people who doggedly write or make art and are good at it will, surely, be published somewhere eventually. Why 'cult figure', 'hero' and the rest of it?

In the 1950s there weren't many places to turn if you wanted to get your story or poem published. Charles Brasch's *Landfall* was the place to be, but it was very highbrow, Literary with a capital L, and not everything matched Brasch's rarefied standards. Sometimes, says Maurice Gee when I visit him and his wife Margareta in Nelson, it seemed like there was nowhere to go, especially if you were just starting out. Eventually Gee became the book-award-hogging novelist we know him as now, but back then he was sending his short stories off hopefully, just like everybody else.

There had been other 'little magazines' that tried to challenge *Landfall*'s dominance, says Gee – Noel Hoggard's *Arena*; something called *Image*; Baxter and Louis Johnson started *Numbers* – but usually they folded pretty fast. So when Dad took over *Mate* at its second issue, and managed to produce another 12 alongside assistant editor Tony Stones before handing it on to another editor, he was 'giving us a place to publish'. To say he was 'keeping writing alive in New Zealand' might seem corny, Gee says, 'but that's not too far off the truth'. Brasch, by founding *Landfall* back in 1947, had been of huge importance, and 'Bob Dudding – I wouldn't say he was a satellite; he was a different star . . . what do you call those things? Twin stars? I've used it in a novel somewhere. An astronomical term . . .'

Binary stars?

'Yes. Binary stars.'

When Dad was being sized up for his honorary doctorate at Auckland University in 2007, Gee wrote one of the letters of commendation.

'It's no exaggeration,' he wrote, 'to call him the (youthful) father of a generation (my generation) of New Zealand writers.'

Not just Gee's generation. From the late 1960s, in *Landfall* and then in *Islands*, Dad was an enthusiastic backer of baby-boomer poet and author Ian Wedde, seeing him as the vanguard of something new and important.

I meet Ian in a café around the corner from his apartment in Ponsonby. He has a walking stick because of an old hip injury, but he's just as groovy and fizzing with energy as I remember from when I was a kid. 'One of the big debts I owe Robin,' he says, 'is that he endorsed the belief that you could put writing at the centre of your life and do a bunch of other stuff – be a postie, or give talks or whatever you had to – to make up the difference. Not just me: he gave a lot of people that signal that yes you can, that it wasn't just a childish whim.'

Underneath the warm encouragement there was discipline. Robin would be reading for the literary business – *What is this about? Is it substantial?* – but he was also doing the close reading: looking for crummy sentences, unnecessary words.

'He was never very intrusive, but he did make some very firm suggestions when it came to the detail of the writing – "too many fucking adjectives", that kind of thing. He burnt a track through how I wrote.'

Ian visited the Duddings in Auckland in the mid-1970s. At that time Dad was editing *Islands* out of a draughty, leaky-roofed shed in the garden that was stuffed to overflowing with mountains of submissions and proofs and other hoarded papers.

Between our house and our neighbours' there was just a straggly hedge, through which Ian and Robin could hear a fractious baby at 2 Sealy Road.

'I remember Robin running through a gap in the hedge and running back through holding this child – he'd obviously totally kidnapped the child – and beginning to cram fish and yoghurt into it. And then he ran back with it through the hedge, and the child was quiet.

'That gap in the hedge stood for a lot. The image I have of Robin running through while clutching this child – it feels to me very like what he did with young writers. He kind of bolted through the hedge and brought them back into the shed, and maybe they were quiet for a while.'

He was still dashing through the hedge and helping young writers a decade later and more. After Beth Nannestad sent him some poems in the late 1970s for consideration for *Islands* he scooped them up and told her she was good. In the early 80s he informed her it was time to publish a collection, and told her who to talk to, where to go, how to do it.

'I owe him me being a poet,' Beth tells me. 'If it hadn't been for the presence of *Islands*, and then that feeling of being under his wing like one of his little chickens, and being told quite succinctly what to do – if it wasn't for that, such poetry as I've written wouldn't have been written.'

Literary magazines, with their miscellanies of poems, stories, reviews, essays and images, can be bitsy, uneven things. Yet I am repeatedly told that Robin Dudding's were always more than the sum of their parts, that they had a shape and logic that made them much more than a grab-bag of the first 15 printable things through the letterbox slot.

Bill Manhire is in the UK teaching a semester at the University of East Anglia, so we talk on Skype.

'The great thing about him as an editor,' says Bill, as I watch his blurry, time-lagged face peering into his laptop from a London hotel room, 'but also his downfall in some ways, was that he waited patiently until work came in. He'd commission essays and reviews and so on too, but there was some organic growth to each issue of *Landfall* that he did, and each issue of *Islands*. He'd decide what fitted and how to order it, without doing one of those heavy-handed thematised issues, which never works. He'd produce an issue that had its own integrity.'

Gregory O'Brien – artist, poet, author, curator and someone who gets more infectiously excited about art and culture than anyone I've ever met – says the Dudding magazines were structured in the same way that a good curator might order an art exhibition: 'setting up the juxtapositions and transitions and the disruptions and disjunctions' between different elements.

The point, says Greg, as he paces around his kitchen in the Wellington suburbs and makes too many coffees for both of us on a stovetop espresso maker, is that editing of the kind Robin did was a creative process of its own. It didn't matter that he wasn't a writer or poet himself.

'Robin was a cult figure really, and it's pretty amazing to be that – having a literary reputation apart from being a practitioner.'

That rare status of non-writing editor was something to which Robin was temperamentally suited, reckons Bill. In his publications there was 'the feeling that Robin was always dashing out of the frame. He wanted to be a presence and take charge, but he always wanted to be an invisible figure', a bit like the description of Stephen Dedalus at the end of Joyce's *A Portrait of the Artist as a Young Man*, as the godlike figure who 'remains within or behind or beyond or above his handiwork, invisible, refined out of existence, indifferent, paring his fingernails'.

The family's hippyish idyll in Christchurch was part of that, says Bill.

'One of the things Robin was doing with his editing was

building a community of writers of which he was the secret chief, the guru, the leader of the commune.

'And that community was alongside that utopian family that I met in Christchurch, but also overlapped with it a bit, because a lot of those writers became family friends and were defeated at ping-pong.'

In a 1991 interview with the poet and journalist Iain Sharp, Bill said getting one of his poems into *Landfall*, not long after Dudding had taken over from Brasch, was a rite of passage, a huge symbolic moment. 'It meant somehow you really were a writer.'

The kudos was as much about the magazine as its new editor, but after Dad was fired and started *Islands* he carried that status – and the loyalty of many of the *Landfall* writers – off with him. The mana was attached to *Islands* still by the time he published Beth Nannestad for the first time.

'If you were good, you could be in *Islands*,' says Beth. 'And it meant you *were* good, this *was* a poem – it wasn't just trying to be. It meant a lot.'

Robin was always waiting for the next great thing to arrive in the mail, says Beth, but he was also having an effect on the world, like a lighthouse – he 'made other people better, because you knew there was someone who was the centre of something, who could tell the difference'.

Mike Beveridge, another baby-boomer writer who was published by Dad in *Landfall* then *Islands* and befriended the family in Christchurch, tells me the Dudding mission to publish wasn't just about supporting or gratifying would-be writers and poets. There was a grander civilising project underway.

Mike, who was once a fairly serious rugby player, has a

vivid memory of going to a test match with Dad in the late 60s or early 70s. They were on the embankment at Lancaster Park, east of the city centre, and as usual it was bedlam.

'There were people pissing on each other and throwing pies into the crowd. And Robin looked at it all, and said, "Imagine parodying this."

'Because that was life. That was the kind of crass, brutal, six-o'clock-closing-get-pissed-and-beat-the-wife life we'd grown up with.

'And he was doing his bit to give us some culture. What a noble thing to have done. What a great thing to have done. You could have done much worse with your life than that.'

Robin Dudding battled the philistines on one front and the snobs on another. Beveridge, who'd grown up in provincial towns around the North Island, found the conservatism, the fake Englishness, the old-boys'-club atmosphere of Christchurch, where he was a PhD student and tutor in the university English department, stultifying. 'I couldn't abide that Christ's College aspect to it – the snobbishness and the twittishness.'

It was wonderful, then, to encounter Robin, someone who would talk seriously about art and language and culture, but didn't feel the need to give himself airs and graces and a false British accent while doing so, and who also knew the score of the latest All Blacks game. There was loose talk, in the early 1970s, between the Duddings and Beveridges about the prospect of founding a small commune in Nelson, but nothing came of it.

Patrick Evans, who was a friend and colleague of Mike, remembers Robin being 'very clear about the New Zealand thing. He said be clear that you write your fiction in New

Zealand and not a fake version of somewhere else, like Pommy-land or the United States.'

By the late 1960s the world was shifting on its axis: Civil Rights in the US, the Vietnam War, the Prague Spring, May '68 in Paris, the hippy movement, feminism and, more locally, the growth of Māori activism. New Zealand often felt a year or two off the pace, but the changing of the guard at *Landfall* in 1967 felt like another tiny symptom of the changing times.

In 1970 the young Māori writer Witi Ihimaera arrived at Robin's offices in Christchurch to ask why he hadn't received a response to stories he'd submitted to *Landfall*, and made his point clearer by pulling out a taiaha and performing a warrior's challenge on the steps of the Caxton Press. Robin waited patiently, then Witi said 'Kia ora' and they went inside to talk. A chapter of what would become Witi's first (and award-winning) novel *Tangi* appeared in *Landfall* later that year.

By 1972 Witi was becoming a literary celebrity with the success of his collection *Pounamu Pounamu*, but his 1973 story 'Clenched Fist' which was published in *Islands*, marked his turn towards darker, more political themes.

When I meet Witi for a coffee in Ponsonby he tells me about his dramatic first meeting with Robin, and how he was always grateful to him for making him visible 'at the highest level'. Even though Robin was supportive, he didn't mince words when rejecting weaker material, chiding Witi when he though he was overdoing things, or being melodramatic, or boring, or superficial. They hatched a plan to work together on a book of modern retellings of Māori myths, but it never quite happened.

For poet and author Fiona Kidman, it seemed Robin was a turning point. He was declaring a new kind of literature that was more inclusive of younger people, of Māori and of women.

She'd been 'knocking on *Landfall*'s door for years, and I'd been getting these cool little notes from Charles Brasch – "Not quite for us" sort of thing. Then Robin took over and the first story I sent him he published.'

He was a few years ahead of the pack in his support of women. It wasn't till 1975 that you saw a 'great blooming' of women writers here, Kidman says, and that was because canny publishers noticed the UN had declared it International Women's Year and suddenly started accepting more work by women. There were nine poetry collections by women published that year, more than in the entire previous decade.

The literary world could feel 'very sexist', especially among the older men, but Kidman saw Robin as 'being the younger man, who was supporting the emergence of women's writing'. This wasn't tokenism – it was about recognising that good stuff could come from anywhere and anyone.

Spotting the good stuff, everyone I speak to agrees, was Robin Dudding's superpower: he had a semi-mystical knack for sorting the wheat from the chaff.

'Nobody can pick things like Robin could,' says Beth Nannestad. 'Nobody.'

He had 'terrific insight into what worked and what didn't', says Kevin Ireland. That's why Bob decided so definitively not to be a writer himself, 'because he could apply that insight to himself as well'. Kevin suspects Dad's time as a reporter gave him an edge: 'Bob came in with a shit-detector to start with, but also a ruthless journalist's ability just to put a pencil through something.'

‘Robin had an eye for good writing,’ says C.K. Stead when I visit him at his Remuera home, where he shows me the framed original of the Peter Siddell drawing Dad commissioned for the cover of *Islands* 25 then gave to Stead after printing, seeing it was an illustration of Stead’s poem ‘Scoria’. ‘He recognised good from less good, and good from bad.’

There was no pedantic aesthetic manifesto at work, says Bill Manhire. The goal was simply ‘print what’s good’. Which also meant there were no free passes based on reputation or friendship. ‘He turned people down happily if he didn’t think it was good enough. Everybody who was established in New Zealand had the experience of being turned down by Robin Dudding. I did.’

With the total control he exerted over *Islands* in particular, he could take some editorial risks, such as turning over the entirety of *Islands* 16 to Wedde’s novel *Dick Seddon’s Great Dive* (which won the 1977 national book award for fiction), or devoting an entire issue to Frank Sargeson in 1978.

‘That sense of focus, and not knowing what the next issue might do, was pretty exciting for subscribers and readers,’ says Bill.

I’d be lying if I said I’ve made exhaustive efforts to track down someone who can give me a contrary view, but there’s an article that appeared in Auckland’s *Metro Magazine* in 1984 which did have a stab at playing devil’s advocate.

Islands was just about to relaunch after a three-year hiatus, and *Metro* writer Robert Mannion headed out to Torbay to meet the man whom someone had pointed out to him as ‘the backbone of the country’s literature for the last 20 years’.

The piece is framed as a spirited discussion about the emperor's new literature – a jolly joust between the no-bullshit journo and the establishment editor who is complacently presiding over an industry-wide circle-jerk. But reading between the lines you get the impression the editor found some of the journalist's questions foolish or naïve, and played a dead bat:

> Tell Dudding modern short stories are quiet and lack guts and he tells you about the quiet ones that work and the ones that are not quiet.
>
> Tell him there are too many academics in New Zealand writing and he points to the writers who are not academics and the academics who are good.
>
> Tell him about the bad writers, and he will not get drawn at all. He does not talk about good or bad writing, only writing he is fond or not so fond of.

But the article attacks not so much Dudding or his magazines as the entire New Zealand literary scene. Mannion quotes snippets from well-known writers to demonstrate that New Zealand literary writing is incomprehensible, its writers self-satisfied, its supporters snobbish. He is withering about NZ Lit's cosy circles of mutual congratulation and its unseemly reverence for its heroes, as exemplified by that 1978 Sargeson-themed issue of *Islands*. 'No one,' claims Mannion, 'should have so much praise heaped upon them.'

Mannion doesn't explain what's wrong with lavish praise, beyond a peevish admission that it makes him want to find fault in Sargeson's work. His specific objections to Sargeson's writing include his use of the words 'categorical imperative' in a story, as if basic vocabulary from Philosophy 101 were the height of pretension.

He concedes that literary magazines 'exist to nurture new talent rather than sell the work of established names' and that *Islands*' peak circulation of 2000 is more than decent compared with similar magazines abroad, yet he still reckons 'the marketplace is some sort of judge', so asks: would *Islands*' circulation be less tiny 'if it was better?'

Even though he sounds like the person who comes out of their first modern art exhibition saying 'My kid could do that', Mannion is nibbling at the edges of some serious and legitimate questions: How *do* you tell what's good and what's not? Who *is* qualified to judge? What Mannion doesn't seem to realise is that it's precisely those puzzles that preoccupy the literary insiders he's scoffing at. Sure, lots of people think Sargeson was terribly important, and he's one of a few names – Mansfield, Baxter and Frame are some of the others – who have achieved mythic status. But there's far more disagreement and bitching about worth and status within the literary bubble than there is outside it.

It's woven through the decades of correspondence I've been skimming in the Turnbull Library: Who's actually good? How do we know? Who am I to say? Have you seen Shadbolt's godawful new novel?

The most vigorous challenges to Dudding's supposed editorial discernment came from writers themselves. In August 1962, James K. Baxter wrote to explain why he would no longer be contributing to *Mate* magazine, which was by that time nine issues old.

He said he was disturbed 'by what seem to me extraordinary errors in your editorial judgement'. He had discovered that, of late, *Mate* had rejected a first-rate poem by Erik Schwimmer and a fine poem by Peter Bland. *Mate* had also returned Baxter's own 'Remuera Housewife' poem, without seeming to realise that it would be a very good complement to the 'Takapuna Businessman' poem which had been accepted.

These blunders led Baxter to conclude 'that you are out of touch with the present development of New Zealand verse, and that your judgement as an editor is deteriorating. I am sorry about this.' *Mate*, it would appear, was becoming too 'established', and its editor was suffering a 'hardening of the mental arteries'.

A month later, delayed by 'sickness and unexpectedly early childbirth', Dad replied, not quite apologetically. He had no intention, he said, 'of eating humble pie', yet the fact was that 'I am in the position of having less respect for my own judgement than I have for yours [. . .] even if it doesn't mean that I always do or will agree with you.'

Anyone, he said, is 'fully entitled to lose faith in an editor if it is thought his or their judgement is consistently wrong [. . .] But still I think the major judgement of luckless editors must be made in the first instance on what is published rather than what is rejected.'

In any case, he wrote, 'fallibility is not a sign of hardening of arteries – we are not less likely to make a mistake now [than] we were 3 years ago.'

Within the week Baxter replied: 'I am a cantankerous old bastard. Even before receiving your letter, I had regretted the smart-aleck acrimonious quality of my last one to you: a scoring-of-points rather than a human communication. I apologise for being like that.'

He said he was saving up most of his verse for a new book,

but 'if I have something I want to send to MATE I'll send it; and if you want it, you'll take it, and if not, then not; and we will both be at peace, as usual. Your letter has taught me better thinking and better manners. That is one gain.'

He was true to his word. In Dad's final, bumper, issue of *Mate* in 1966, the first seven pages were given over to poems by Baxter.

As Bill Manhire recalls it, Robin was very clear in his judgement when something was bad. He was less clear when something was good. His views on prose were more confident when it was realistic than when surrealistic. He wasn't always sure what the younger poets he encountered from the 1970s onwards were up to, and would sometimes seek a second opinion.

'Occasionally,' says Bill, 'he would send me something secretively and say, "Here's something by famous writer X and I want to print it, but there's something wrong with it. Do you have a sense of that?" And sometimes I did and sometimes I didn't.'

It's something Bill has tried to explain to his creative writing students at Victoria University, that a really good editor has all sorts of responses to a work. They don't just look at it and say 'that's rubbish' or 'that's wonderful'. 'They approach it from all sides if they're doing their job properly. So don't assume that an editor knows better than you. They're fallible.'

In 2003 Bill enticed Dad out of retirement to edit the annual *Best New Zealand Poems* online series, selected from works published in collections and literary magazines the previous year.

In a rather lovely introductory essay Dad wrote about the difficulty, the folly, of choosing just 25 poems and calling them the 'best'. There seemed to be two selection approaches, he wrote: 'attempt to find worthwhile examples of as wide a range of poetic expression as possible, or plump for the poems that you like best, even if there is the risk of too markedly revealing one's own taste or lack of taste'.

He took the latter option, and if the fallibility this ensured wasn't obvious enough, there was always the quote he put at the top of the essay, from someone called Fabricius: 'Let certainty be tempered with disbelief.'

Another thing keeps coming up in these interviews – Dad's constant willingness to pay an unreasonable personal cost while pursuing his quixotic goals, or while serving the nation's literature, or whatever it was he was doing.

He kept making these magazines despite being desperately short of time (especially in the early days when he edited alongside working fulltime and fathering an improbably large family) and desperately short of money (especially in the *Islands* years when editing became the principal pursuit and our family finances ebbed ever lower) and despite being driven to the brink of panic and despair with every issue.

Mike Beveridge sees it as heroic altruism. 'He was willing to be supportive of anybody and to sacrifice his own wellbeing to do so. When [poet] Bob Orr and I talk about Robin we always describe him as a hero.'

In Gee's letter of recommendation for Dad's doctorate he wrote: 'Editors don't become famous. They work quietly, often in difficult circumstances, but the best of them deserve to be recognised as cultural heroes. Robin Dudding is in this class.'

Stead, who also wrote a very nice letter of recommendation, tells me that his admiration was often mixed with exasperation. He found it hard to watch as the notorious Dudding slowness morphed into something more pathological, as submissions disappeared into a black hole for months or years and the arrival of the latest *Islands* slipped ever further out of sync with the date printed on the spine.

'I was always sympathetic to the fact that he was short of money all the time and struggling along, so in that sense I saw it as heroic. But you can't go on being heroic in slow motion. Eventually the heroism aspect dies, and what you're watching is something running out of steam.'

I like the way Patrick Evans puts it during a long phone conversation – me in Auckland, him in Christchurch – partly because Patrick's version makes me laugh, but also because it most closely matches my own impression that there was a self-defeating urge at the heart of many of Dad's endeavours.

'It seemed to me,' says Patrick, 'that he was on that borderline between creativity and destructiveness, and all the good things that he did came out of a sea of chaos'. The chaos was evident both at home in Barnes Road, and in the office at the Caxton Press where *Landfall* was being edited.

When you visited him at Barnes Road, 'he'd be hacking the weeds down helplessly, and trying to plant the vegetables and get them watered, and there was never enough time to quite do enough watering'. The Caxton office meanwhile was famously messy, filled with box after box after box of correspondence.

'The boxes were sort of a joke. He'd come in and say, "I've been trying to clear the boxes and as a result there are 10 more of the bloody things."

'One of the reasons his time and motions were so bad, why he was inefficient, was that so many people would come into his office and he'd never turn them away. You'd go there and there'd be would-be writers and real writers – it was a bit of a salon. But he'd never be looking at his watch and saying, "Oh I've only got 10 minutes." So I don't think he ever got on top of the job.

'You'd go in and he'd say, "Oh I'm in the shit. I don't think I'm going to get this issue out", and he'd be crashing around looking panicky – and then the issue would come out and it would be terrific. He was a terrific editor.'

'Robin Dudding is a very important figure in New Zealand writing,' said Bill Manhire in his 1991 interview with Iain Sharp, 'and at some stage someone will have to sit down and try to work out just what his presence consists of, apart from the considerable beard.'

Fair enough, but I think it's important not to underestimate the beard itself. I track down an email address for Richard Herring – half of the comedy duo who took the piss out of Dad for 40 seconds on a BBC TV sketch show a decade and a half ago. What, I ask Herring, was that all about?

Herring remembers the 'Men of Achievement 1974' gag fondly. He and his comedy partner Stewart Lee found the book and were amused 'partly by the 70s fashions, partly because we assumed people had paid to be featured, partly because with the passage of years being a man of achievement in 1974 is a bit of a double-edged sword'. As a recurring gag it didn't last long, because no one really liked it as much as Herring and Lee did.

To the best of Herring's recollection, the person they

zoomed in on each week was chosen based on an amusing picture or because of their listed hobbies.

'I would therefore suspect that your father's beard was the cause of his inclusion.'

10. Lean and hungry

I'M BARELY in the door, still fumbling to get my digital recorder out of my satchel, when the words start tumbling out of Tom McWilliams – a torrent of memories and theories and digressions, interrupted only by his wonderful roaring giggle or by his occasional stammer, which is of the kind that brings you to the balls of your feet, wide-eyed as to where his sentence is going to go next.

Tom is retired, 75ish. I guess he's been thinking about Robin Dudding, and his intersections with him over 50-odd years, ever since I emailed three days earlier and invited myself to his house in Westmere, Auckland.

I follow Tom into the kitchen, where he's making tea, or rather, clattering cups and fiddling with the kettle switch and absently swinging a teabag in the air, too caught up in what he's saying to take the final step of lowering it into a cup.

Tom was at Teachers' Training College around 1959 when he befriended Tony Stones, who like him was planning to become an art teacher. Tony introduced Tom to his cronies

Kevin Ireland and Robin Dudding. Tony, Kevin and Robin were a tight trio – the artist, the poet, the editor. Tony and Kevin were the showmen, the big presences, says Tom. They were the Lennon and McCartney, but Robin was quiet, the one who stood shyly to one side.

Tom notices the teabag dangling from his hand, then looks back up and locks me in his gaze. 'Robin was *George Harrison*,' he says wonderingly, as if slightly surprised by his own analogy.

When the tea's finally made and we're sitting at a sunny table in the corner of the sitting room, Tom tries to recall his first impressions of Robin. He didn't know him terribly well back then; it wasn't till decades later that they became close while working at the *Listener*.

'In the early days with Robin, I thought he might be a bit slow. When I met him with Lois I thought now *there's* the brains of the outfit. He talked very little, and when he talked it was very softly. He didn't try to sell anything.'

Here's another way of putting it, says Tom, who is not only a Beatles fan but a film buff. Think about the 50s and 60s. 'Who were the heroes? Who were the guys you wanted to be like? This sounds ridiculous, but it's the Western hero – the laconic guy who's actually going to deliver the goods but he's not selling anything, and he's a bit of a mystery man.

'Isn't that Robin?' says Tom. 'The slightly downcast look' – he jumps from his chair and adopts a marksman stance – 'you can almost see him sighting down the barrel. There's a core in there, but a surface that doesn't give anything away. Robin was like that.'

I rather like the idea of Dad as The Man with No Name,

sweeping into a no-good town, cleaning things up with a few salvos of poems and critical essays, then skipping town without saying goodbye, leaving hearts broken and closed minds prised open. Better, surely, than being George Harrison.

Kevin left Auckland in 1959. The remaining pair, Tony and Robin, were only five years older than Tom, but the gap felt bigger than that to him. They were *men*. They had wives and mortgages and children. They lived in poverty-stricken bohemia with jam jars for tumblers. They had artistic purpose. They were making a magazine.

All true. But these things were also pretty new to Robin. He'd barely finished being that kid who slept on a park bench and hitch-hiked to Cambridge to visit a girl he fancied.

He was 22 when he married in March 1958. His first magazine, *Mate* 2, the one he'd co-edited with Dave Walsh and with the cover illustration by Tony, came out in November the same year. My oldest sister Rachel was born the following month ('definitely a first-night effort', as Dad over-shared in a letter to his mother announcing the pregnancy). By his 24th birthday he'd trained as a primary school teacher and quit journalism, and a second baby was on the way.

At the end of 1960 the family of four moved into the old two-bedroom house in Torbay they'd bought for £2000, and it wasn't long before the garden was dug, the first chicken coop was installed and Lois was pregnant again. Books, chooks, tomatoes, kids – apart from the beard, which wouldn't arrive in earnest until 1973, the defining characteristics of Robin Dudding were all in place. Dad kept the traveller Kevin Ireland encyclopaedically updated on the fate of *Mate* and the continuing adventures of the Queen's Ferry crowd, even if the demands of teaching and domestic life, and the remoteness of Torbay, meant his contact with the scene had become intermittent.

In May 1961 he told Kevin about one of his rare sorties to town for an exhibition opening, at which 'anyone who was anyone was there'.

'As I usually get rotten and disgrace myself at any such formal functions, I was very carefully only slowly sipping the watered-down plonk when down the stairs, much bandaged, slid Abungus [Barry] Crump.'

Crump, it turned out, had crashed a truck loaded with dogs in Taupo and ended up in hospital, from where he had only recently made his escape. On a whim he'd bought himself a new car and driven up to Auckland.

Almost everyone, wrote Robin, was overjoyed at Crump's arrival. Crump 'managed in a short time to deposit all likely males down at this brand-new car with a few bottles of 4X, and ducked back to entrap most of the eligible females in the lavatory from where emerged all sorts of interesting sounds'.

Crump's sex life and finances were a source of constant fascination for the Auckland literary set, who'd taken in this rough-as-guts bloke from the backblocks, given him a few tips for polishing up his pub yarns and getting them on paper, then realised they had a bestselling celebrity in their midst. Sightings of the prodigal bushman were passed along the grapevine, such as this letter from Jack Lasenby to Dad from January 1962: 'Maurice said he saw Crump in Wellington last week. He has the latest in Landrovers and flashy guitars and seems to be picking up a few prestige fucks.'

In a 1965 letter, Dad told Kevin he'd just 'devoured' the first novel by Jean Watson, the writer who'd introduced him to Lois. The book, *Stand in the Rain*, is a lightly fictionalised first-person account of Jean's early relationship with Crump, at which time Crump was still married and occasionally returning to his wife. In the book Crump becomes 'Abungus' (not such a heavy disguise, given that Abungus was what his friends called him anyway) and Jean becomes the narrator 'Sarah'.

The novel, Dad told Kevin, was 'very good', even if it contained an 'accurate if unflattering portrait of yours truly'.

Now that's intriguing. I get *Stand in the Rain* out of the stack section of the library and skim it in search of a fictionalised Dad. Presumably he'll have a different name, but I figure I'll still spot him: maybe he's there as Abungus's first publisher, or as a chicken-raising schoolteacher. Perhaps Jean has written about the day she introduced Lois and Robin.

But no luck. I read the whole book and can't spot him.

Then I come across another letter from Wellington, this time from Maurice Gee, sent to Dad in 1958. Amid the updates about mutual friends, Moss said he'd run into Jean Watson, 'who said you'd turned her out of your home just for committing adultery. She seemed genuinely puzzled.'

Bingo! That's just like a scene from *Stand in the Rain*. Sarah and Abungus are asked by a character called Rex Potter to leave his house after he learns they've restarted their affair even though Abungus has supposedly returned to his wife, Dell.

So Rex must be Robin. And he seems something of a puritan:

Rex Potter was not at all pleased to see this reviving of a relationship which he considered based on escapism and fantasy. Abungus was being particularly loving, too, and at everything nice he said to me Rex would frown with disapproval.

After tea Abungus said that he was in love with me not Dell and we were off to Wellington and that we ought to go out and tell her. Rex took me aside and said, 'I think you better leave. It'd be all right if you were here on your own or with Jerry, but under these circumstances I think you better leave.'

'Why?'

'It's nothing personal. You know we're always pleased to see you on your own, either of you, but both together . . .'

So we went – 'It's nothing personal don't forget,' Rex called after us.

Rex was doing the right thing by his standards. I admire him now for saying what he thought and not harbouring people who he considered were doing the wrong thing. He was being loyal to Dell. It is always so much easier to keep thoughts like that to yourself. At the time we were both hurt and indignant. Rex had always been a close friend of mine.

It's an odd little anecdote. Mum doesn't remember anything resembling it, but perhaps she wasn't there, or Dad didn't tell her at the time why their friends had left in a hurry.

His unwelcome high-mindedness caused no serious rift with Crump. Crump had another story in *Mate* 4, but after that he was getting too big for literary mags. He responded to Dad's request for him to give *Mate* a plug from his pedestal of newfound fame like this:

Why the fucking hell do you presume I should acknowledge your scoury-arsed magazine in my immortal works? Mate, according to a recent letter from someone whose opinion you value, should acknowledge my contribution to it – "Your story in "Mate" is the best thing it has come up with to date, and, in itself, justifies the magazine's existence!" (unquote)

I'll swap you a review copy of my book for a couple of free "Mates". (A profit for you of 10/-)

Sorry I can't let you have any stuff at present. Have just finished second book (Watch Reed's 1961 publishing list) and am unable to bring myself to even think about any more writing for a while. I've run out of bullshit. [. . .]

Still hard up, hunting and hounded by the Police. In & out of jail like a berserk shuttle. The country's fucked for the want of more literary magazines.

Regs. to Lois & kid(s)
Forever Yours,
Crump.

'I have nothing but regard and pity for Barry,' wrote Dad in a letter to Kevin. 'Like Schulberg's character* he is a public figure – N.Z. hasn't had one before and is forever expected to act the part of the swanee-ed deer stalker – bloody awful for him. But he is pretty resilient I think.'

* Probably Budd Schulberg's 1941 book *What Makes Sammy Run* about a screenwriter who rises from the mean streets to the top of Hollywood, selling his soul along the way.

Editing and publishing was the grand project, but to feed his growing horde, Dad taught. As best as I can tell he clashed with headmasters, alienated school inspectors and was loved by his pupils, especially Standards One and Two at Browns Bay School, who in 1965 spent most of a term building a life-sized papier-mâché cow called Strawberry, who was the star exhibit of the East Coast Bays Art and Music Festival. 'I'm a terrible teacher,' he told his mother in a letter.

He used the back of some of his classroom notes to take carbon copies of his outgoing *Mate* correspondence, which is why I know that in February 1964 a boy called Philip hit a girl on the jungle gym and later 'cried because didn't want his T. Bear "poked" at Dolls Show'. Philip's classmates, meanwhile, are noted as variously 'chatty', 'annoying', and 'Sent back from swimming for throwing seaweed'.

Through the 1960s *Mate* ticked along, albeit at a gradually slowing pace: three issues in 1960, two apiece in 1961 and 62; one a year for the next four years. Tony remained assistant editor even after he got a senior job in the design department at TVNZ; on Friday evenings Dad would come into the city and they'd work through the latest submissions in the TVNZ cafeteria till late.

Mate 4, published in February 1960, contained a section devoted to Māori writers, including Hone Tuwhare and Mason Durie. There was excitement in 1963 when poems by Louis Johnson and Peter Hooper were deemed indecent and pulled at the last minute. In a letter to Johnson, Dad explained that 'the printer sent these two poems to his solicitor who while he admitted not to getting a hard on and to having no feeling of having been corrupted [. . .] told the printers they were not to print them etc etc'. *Mate*'s circulation peaked at around 1000 copies and with the help of grants from the Literary Fund almost broke even.

In 1964 Dad dared dream of a career in populist publishing when Mate Books published Barry Mitcalfe's *Salvation Jones*, a book of humorous Crump-esque yarns about a hard-living Kiwi hard case. Dad borrowed money from his father to print it, became euphoric when the first print run of 3000 (distributed, like *Mate*, from Sealy Road's dining table) sold out, but even after selling another 1500 from a second run of 2000, somehow he made no money. A 1965 poetry collection by Peter Bland, *My Side of the Story*, was a proper disaster, selling 300 copies and leaving him £250 in the red (almost $10,000 in today's money).

In other words, Dad's lifelong inability to make money was firmly established early on. He wasn't innumerate. It's just that whenever he made his financial projections he'd make sure contributors and printers were going to get paid and that readers wouldn't be asked to spend too much, and if that meant there was going to be nothing (or less than nothing) left over to pay himself, he'd go ahead regardless and make a financial loss, then moan about the miseries of poverty.

Tom McWilliams was giving Crump a ride home from the pub once, and they got talking about Robin and money. Tom said, 'Well, you know Robin's really been paying to do *Mate*', and Crump said, 'Well, more fool him.'

Crump had, after all, dedicated *A Good Keen Man* 'To LSD' (pounds, shillings and pence), but such straightforward enthusiasm for wealth was unusual among that crowd. Tom thinks that, like a lot of them, Robin 'believed that money was evil. He wouldn't have taken a vow of poverty, but subconsciously I think he did. It's that socialist thing – people with a lot of money are bent; they're not honest like us.'

Being a starving artist was a competitive sport in the literary set. 'My wife is convinced,' Dad wrote to the novelist Noel Hilliard in 1960, 'that our wolves, for lean and hungry looks, would knock yours for a row of ashcans.'

In a 1965 letter he bragged to Barry Mitcalfe:

> The Duddings live as ever. Sample conversation overhead today to show you how the side is being let down.
>
> Neighbours snotty-nosed brat: Rachel why haven't youse got any carpets in your place?
>
> Rachel: Dad was saying he might be getting some soon.
>
> NSNB: We have.
>
> No copyright required as a germ for best-selling poem.

He saved his most honest complaints for his long-distance confidant Kevin Ireland. 'Christ I hate this poverty,' he wrote just after Christmas 1961. 'Imagine £10 a week for the last 2 1/2 years as teacher's salary.'

In a letter to Kevin in April 1964, he unleashed the full force of his self-doubt and existential dread:

> Dear Kevin,
>
> I don't know what the hell to say to you. My neglect depresses me so much that I can't raise the energy to make excuses. This country is just getting too bloody – too enervating – somehow all one's energies, hopes, wishes, desires are sucked away – I've always felt snail-shells emptied of the meat by God-knows-what soft-mouthed sucker are forlorn objects. I'm one [. . .]

Both Lois and [Tony Stones' wife] Cushla are to borrow a Crumpism in possession of belly-fulls of arms and legs. Woe is us. The house is falling down with dry rot, wet rot, financial rot and creeping paralysis and so life goes on.

Kevin responded by asking Robin if he'd heard of the pill.

A year and a bit later the Dudding finances were in genuine peril. 'If you want to really feel miserable for me,' Dad told Kevin, 'our house mortgage falls due in December of this year – I have no knowledge of how to refinance and find that I owe £1,750 on a house valued at £1800 five years ago'.

In the end he addressed his mortgage problem just like any bohemian offspring of bourgeois parents would: he wrote a letter to his father.

The letters about money between Robin and Ernest Dudding through the 50s and 60s make me wince. It's obvious Robin hated to ask for help, especially from the man who had always rubbed him up the wrong way, and his requests are an odd mix of obsequiousness and aggression, as if he was inviting his father to prove he was a bastard by not stumping up.

'I'm not begging for this,' he wrote, when asking for help with the original Torbay house deposit. 'In many ways I'd sooner not be any more beholden to you.' He still took Ernest's £500 loan.

It was more complicated when, a couple of years later, Ernest underwrote the publication of *Salvation Jones* and got closely involved in the sales, marketing and accounting, probably as a condition of risking his money. Over months of correspondence between Hastings and Auckland the two men circled each other, clearly trying to find common ground and to work together, yet unable to overcome their history and their natures – thin-skinned defensiveness on Dad's part, a streak of subtle cruelty on his father's.

Ernest suggested Dad go about things in a more 'business-like manner' by forming a company alongside him and hiring an accountant. Dad said thanks but no thanks.

When *Salvation Jones* sales tapered off earlier than hoped, Ernest wrote: 'If you take my advice you will not spend more money on advertisements. I think you are only thrashing a dead horse. Actually, your advertising has been excellent really, better than the book warrants.'

Dad was offended. 'You write as if Salvation isn't a success – it is – we've sold over 4000 now – which compares with any other book except Crump published this year. With a little more help from shops we would have sold twice as many. Admittedly I won't make much if anything – but I didn't aim to unless sales were terrific – this one was for experience and costed to break even. There'll be more to come this year.'

In mid-1965 he was back, asking for a large loan to help pay debts from the disastrous Bland poetry collection. 'You – penniless, retired etc etc are my first avenue of escape. I haven't worked out my other avenues yet although I have been noticed hanging around the offices of a South American Airline.'

I'm not sure whether Ernest said yes to the printer bill loan, but it was only a couple of months later that Dad wrote again, asking for help with the mortgage that was about to default, and Ernest bailed him out. That's when he wrote the scolding letter advising Dad not to let children draw on the walls.

Ernest lived another 16 years, but the wariness between them was never resolved.

A couple of months before Grandad died in 1981, Dad and his brother Ian were both in Hastings, and Ian watched in amazement as they re-enacted the sort of argument they might have had when Dad was a teenager – a blazing, pointless, row about a coat.

Ernest had bought a cheap coat by mail order from Hamilton and it didn't fit, so he asked Robin to take it to Hamilton for him on his way home and exchange it. It was a big detour and Robin was short of time, so he refused, and Ernest hit the roof.

'If you can't do that for me,' he yelled, 'I'm doing nothing for you. You're not having that chicken I killed for you! You're not taking any of the fruit out of the garden!'

If he'd asked Ian to do it, Ian would have followed his own childhood script of bending with the breeze. He'd have agreed to exchange the coat then not bothered, or he'd have binned it and bought a new one once he got home.

Robin's principles (and lack of cash) made such slippery solutions unthinkable. He stalked out in a fury and drove home with no coat, no chicken, no fruit. It was possibly the last conversation father and son ever had.

11. Cold south

At 7 o'clock on a wet, cold morning in late August 1966, an ancient, ramshackle little car rolled off the brand new Wellington car-ferry onto Lyttelton wharf, packed to the roof with luggage, blankets, linen and its six travellers: a couple in their early 30s and their four young daughters.

To the man waiting for them on the wharf as they drove off the *Wahine*,* they looked like refugees at journey's end. They'd come a long way and were very tired, but they were cool and quiet in themselves and with their children – no fuss, no impatience, no indulgence. The oldest girl, Rachel, told the man she would be turning eight in December. The youngest, Natasha, looked no older than two.

The family were, the man wrote in his diary that evening, 'obviously very poor'. The father's clothes were 'cheap, & old

* Yes, that *Wahine*. The Scottish-built ferry had been running the Wellingon–Lyttelton route for three weeks. In August 1968 she foundered and capsized in Wellington Harbour, killing 53 people.

& worn'. Yet he had 'a very quiet natural authority, which he is probably unaware of, coming from his inner certainty'.

The man on the wharf was Charles Brasch. As someone with a private income, a beneficiary of the Hallenstein clothing fortune, he probably had high sartorial standards, but no doubt the assessment was spot on. Even when he had money to spare for clothes, Dad never seemed too interested in what he wore.

Halfway through the mile-and-a-bit of road tunnel linking Lyttelton to central Christchurch the refugees' car broke down, but grinding along at 20 miles an hour, they finally made it.

The Duddings had made their unsteady way to the South Island because Brasch had finally found someone to take over the editorship of *Landfall*. Brasch had edited the magazine unpaid from his hometown of Dunedin and it was printed at the Caxton Press in Christchurch, but in order to convert the editorship to a salaried role Caxton had agreed to wrap it into a broader job of 'general editor', which would include some boring commercial work.

Other names had been in the picture – C.K. Stead, Vincent O'Sullivan, Ken Arvidson, Mac Jackson, Tony Kingsbury – but in the end it was Dudding who was able, available and willing to move to Christchurch. The *Mate* baton, meanwhile, was passed to a startled Tom McWilliams, who edited it with the continued assistance of Tony Stones for a few more years.

Brasch's diaries show he'd first sized up Dad for taking over *Landfall* as early as 1960, when *Mate* was only a few issues old. Aucklander Frank Sargeson knew Dudding pretty well, so Brasch asked him for an assessment. Young Dudding, Sargeson informed him, 'is a nice fellow but only just not illiterate'.

Brasch didn't take Sargeson's word for it. He subscribed to *Mate*, struck up a correspondence with Dad, contributed some poems, paid him a few visits. After one visit in 1961 he wrote in his diary that Dudding was 'a young man quietly sure of himself, without worldly ambition or any gnawing wish to be a writer', though it seemed there were 'difficulties of money & time to contend with'. Well spotted.

It might be overdoing the pop psychology to say that in Brasch, 26 years his senior, Dad finally found the supportive father figure he had missed out on by birth. Yet Brasch was his rock throughout the *Landfall* years.

More facilitator than mentor, he didn't tell Robin *how* to edit – he just made it easier for him to do so. He arranged introductions with literary old hands and young talent. He also lent Dad much of the cost of our house in Christchurch, and later wrote off most of the debt.

Dad, for his part, was hugely grateful for Brasch's support, even as he set about jazzing up a magazine which under Brasch had gained a reputation for prissiness and perfectionism, and even though he suspected Brasch disapproved of much of what he published. He was the new broom, but he still wanted the older man's approval. And, unlike Dad's real father, Brasch seemed able to give it wholeheartedly.

Landing the *Landfall* job was a thrill, of course.

'[I] have perhaps,' Dad wrote to Kevin Ireland in shock, 'joined the establishment.'

Yet despite the kudos, and a salary far higher than he got for teaching, and a well-resourced office complete with secretary, despite finally being paid to be an editor rather than squeezing it around an irrelevant day job, despite the relative spaciousness of Woodspring Cottage in Barnes Road after the crowded little Torbay home, and despite the feeling of security that you'd think would come from knowing a very wealthy patron had your back, Dad made heavy weather of it. He hated the dreary Caxton chores that kept him away from *Landfall*, and Christchurch in general weighed him down – the cold, the snobbery of the self-defined gentry, the conservatism, the bitchy, gossipy literary scene.

His patented blend of panicky despair and ironic optimism, and his love of complicatedly punctuated subclauses, is showcased as ever in his confessional letters to Kevin Ireland, like this one from September 1970. (The opening apology is, I think, for being indecisive with some poems Kevin has submitted.)

> How apologise? And how attempt to explain how I'm flogged to death with work, kids, mortgages, bad debts, overgrown wilderness of half-an-acre, house powdering to dust, drainage boards, councils demanding this connection, that money – don't use that septic tank, that well's polluted; how Lf is thrown together desperately late time after time squeezed between the routines of proof-reading, listening to every bastard under the sun who's got a complaint, sub-editing putrid, nonsensical 'histories' by descendants of deckmen from the 'Charlotte Jane' or whatever it was called.* Over the Bridle Path we come again and again; how the book-length manuscripts pile up behind me – all the

* The *Charlotte Jane* was one of the 'first four ships' of English settlers colonising Canterbury, and is seen by some Cantabrians as little short of the *Mayflower*.

poets (and others) who want books out and who I'm too soft-hearted to say 'No' to until I've read them, and sat on them and sat on them hoping for a miraculous new world where everybody who wants work out can achieve this thru Dudding's fleshless hands.

Impossible to explain, so I shan't attempt to. Five kids and another knocking and I don't even have time to sing them 'Kevin Barry' [. . .]

Woe, woe and more woe. We're getting old, but we'll live I think. Spring again here, but the only signs of libido around is the grass growing.

Such wailing – and yet this was also the era of the backyard golf with hockey sticks and craft nights, of Mum up a tree reading her book, of rambunctious family fun. I don't think he was miserable *all* the time. Also, that sixth kid 'knocking' is me – the first Dudding son.

The day I was born, Dad planted a weeping gum in my name in the back garden. A month later there was a 'bottle party' at Barnes Road, for which he made a hand-printed tri-fold invitation featuring old-fashioned illustrations of a double bed† and a giant stork towing a baby in a chariot.

Once unfolded the invitation reads: 'AFTER 13 YEARS OF TRYING; AFTER PRODUCING FIVE AMAZONIAN DAUGHTERS (Rachel, Ruth, Melissa, Natasha, Anna) WE'VE FINALLY HAD (ON BLACK FRIDAY, NOVEMBER 13) *A* SON—ADAM (probably).' A

† Thanks to the compendious knowledge of printer and book-maker Brendan O'Brien, I now know the printer's block of the double bed is the same one used in Caxton's 1967 pamphlet of James K. Baxter's 'A Small Ode on Mixed Flatting', his brilliant response to Otago University's attempt to ban the immoral practice.

footnote reads: 'Men, a bottle will help (the Family Benefit is shot): Ladies, a chastity belt, or similar.'

I have a copy of the original invitation, but there's another in Brasch's papers at the Hocken Library. On Brasch's, Dad has scribbled an apologetic note: 'Tasteless: But just in case you're in town. Regards, Robin.'

I don't know if Brasch made it, but I've still got two of my gifts from that party, during which I reportedly mainly slept. Mike Beveridge, the rugby-playing literature scholar and *Landfall* contributor, turned up with a children's size leather rugby ball, and the artist Ralph Hotere gave an A4 ink sketch of a semi-reclining naked woman – 'an Eve for Adam', he said.

Beveridge's rugby ball is in a box somewhere, squashed flat and wrinkled like a giant dried fig. The Hotere sketch had an even harder life – it spent a couple of decades sellotaped to the walls of Dad's various offices at the mercy of sunlight and fly-shit, another 10 years rolled in a cardboard tube, and then made a long and expensive visit to the paper conservators at Auckland Art Gallery Toi o Tāmaki. They told me they'd repaired a few Hotere sketches of similar vintage, also given as birthday or christening gifts, but none had been as badly mistreated as mine. It's now in a frame in my sitting room, though it's so faded you can barely see what Eve's up to.

The most familiar memento from this part of my life, though, is a black-and-white photo Dad took of Mum breastfeeding me. I'm about four months old and unbelievably fat with heavily dimpled cellulite thighs. Mum and I are both naked, outside in bright sun, though the baby on her lap preserves Mum's modesty a little. Dad liked the picture so much he got it blown up and mounted on a piece of board two foot high. Ever since I could remember, this giant photo of naked Madonna and child sat on our mantelpiece, occasionally overlain by more conventional school photos and holiday snaps.

Some visitors thought it odd, but I never found it embarrassing, partly because for many years I didn't realise what it was showing. Like one of those optical illusions where it's either a candlestick or two faces in profile, I always misread the image. To me the arrangement of shoulders and breasts and baby looked like a slightly deformed rhinoceros roaring into the sky.

Dad's five-and-a-half-year adventure within the establishment came to an end in April 1972, when Caxton's managing director, Dennis 'Dinny' Donovan, suddenly fired him.

Before I'd even looked at the many letters in the Turnbull collections concerning the matter, I discovered that faint, unreliable rumours about the Caxton Dismissal Mystery were still doing the rounds of NZ Lit more than 40 years on.

'Apparently . . .' said someone who was about 10 in 1972 and who must have heard it third-hand at best, Robin had an affair with his boss's wife.

I wasn't in the country at the time, said someone else, 'so all I heard was gossip – the usual things, from a clash of personalities, to sex. I know the gossip but I'm not willing to repeat it. It's all hearsay.'

'I heard there were complaints from Caxton that he was slow in delivery,' said one writer. And wasn't there something about a Katherine Mansfield story making an edition of *Landfall* late?

'I just bought the line everybody was offering,' said another. 'That Donovan had behaved like a horrible man and Robin had been forced to walk away from the whole thing.'

By now I was learning that Dad *did* have an affair (or something resembling one) while he was employed by Caxton – though it certainly wasn't with Donovan's wife. Yet the dalliance had ended almost half a decade earlier and I could see little evidence that it had any direct connection to the sudden sacking.

The truth, then?

Donovan was a wealthy businessman, and by virtue of letting Caxton subsidise low- or no-profit literary publications, he was a patron of the arts and proud to be. But he was also a loudmouth and a bully, a big drinker who liked to rant and swear at his employees, especially after a session at the pub. Maybe he reminded Robin of his father, only worse because of the drinking.

Robin was a perfectionist, a neurotic. He was too slow, too careful, unrealistic about time and money and deadlines, always busting the page limits and budgets set by Donovan. He was much more interested in *Landfall* than the tedious work of the general editor. He was unaffected and honest. He had a natural affinity with writers and artists. He was quietly confident of his judgement. He wasn't a drinker – especially after he developed a stress-related stomach ulcer. He chafed against authority in general and tyrants in particular.

None of these things would have been to Donovan's liking.

The tension between the drunken bully and the thin-skinned neurotic mounted. There were polite professional disagreements but also flare-ups over far pettier things: the time Donovan threatened to fire Robin if he moved a heater in the office; the time Donovan went berserk after Robin

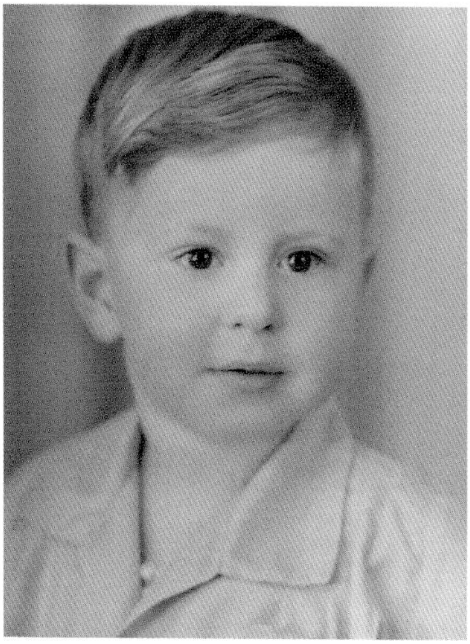

Robin Dudding, around 1938.

Bohemia in Auckland. From left: poet Kevin Ireland, artist Tony Stones and would-be editor Robin Dudding on Queen Street, sometime in the mid-1950s. (Note the ever-present cigarette.)

Robin, centre, with parents Ernest and Winifred, sister Ngaire and brother Ian. The photo was taken the day of Robin and Lois's wedding in March 1958, hence the cat-that-got-the-cream expression, and the ladies' hats.

Robin Dudding and Lois Miller at a party in Auckland, mid-1950s. Robin was instantly drawn to this young woman who reminded him of Ingrid Bergman. She took a while to reciprocate. (Note the ever-present cigarette.)

Mate 2, Robin's first magazine, co-edited with Dave Walsh and with contributors including Barry Crump, Maurice Gee, Frank Sargeson, Kevin Ireland and Lois Miller. The cover drawing by Tony Stones is of George, whom he met while seagulling on the Auckland wharves.

Landfall 84, the fourth Dudding edition of the literary journal founded by Charles Brasch in 1947. The cover design is by Ralph Hotere, and contributors included Michael Gifkins, Ruth Dallas, Frank Sargeson, K. O. Arvidson and Ian Wedde, with paintings by Gretchen Albrecht.

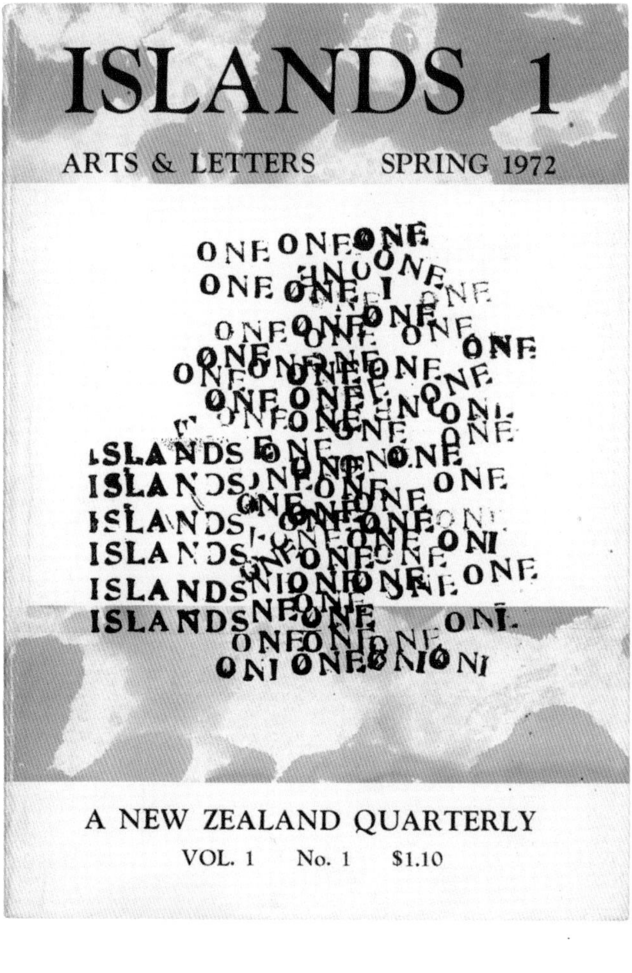

Ralph Hotere's cover design, complete with bilingual dirty joke, for the launch edition of *Islands*, which was founded in the white heat of outrage that followed Robin's dismissal from editorship of *Landfall* and the Caxton Press.

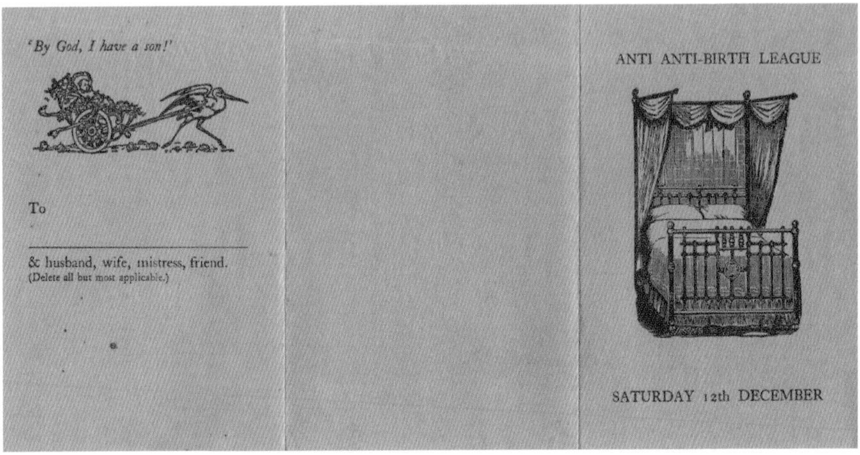

'By God, I have a son!'

To

& husband, wife, mistress, friend.
(Delete all but most applicable.)

ANTI ANTI-BIRTH LEAGUE

SATURDAY 12th DECEMBER

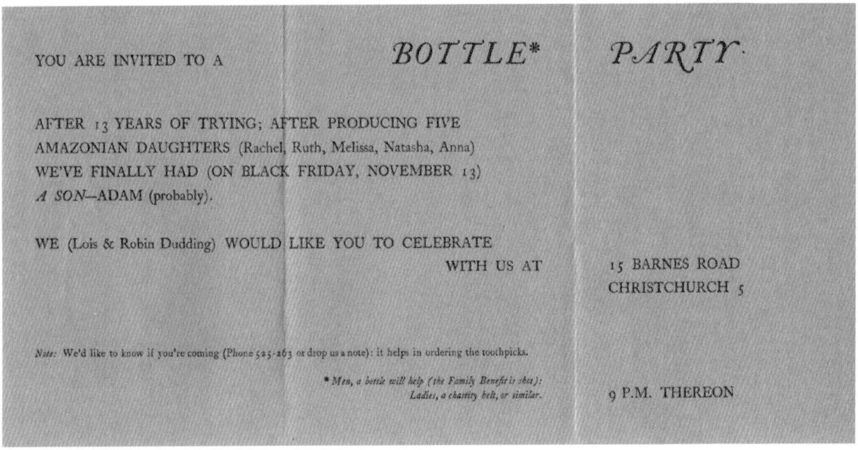

YOU ARE INVITED TO A *BOTTLE** *PARTY*

AFTER 13 YEARS OF TRYING; AFTER PRODUCING FIVE AMAZONIAN DAUGHTERS (Rachel, Ruth, Melissa, Natasha, Anna) WE'VE FINALLY HAD (ON BLACK FRIDAY, NOVEMBER 13) *A SON*—ADAM (probably).

WE (Lois & Robin Dudding) WOULD LIKE YOU TO CELEBRATE WITH US AT

15 BARNES ROAD
CHRISTCHURCH 5

9 P.M. THEREON

Note: We'd like to know if you're coming (Phone 525-263 or drop us a note): it helps in ordering the toothpicks.

* *Men, a bottle will help (the Family Benefit is shot): Ladies, a chastity belt, or similar.*

A party to celebrate the 1970 arrival of the sixth Dudding child. The double-bed image had previously decorated James K. Baxter's subversive 'A Small Ode on Mixed Flatting', which was printed at Caxton Press in 1967.

Lois breastfeeding Adam in the garden at Barnes Road, Christchurch, early 1971. Robin liked the photo so much he ordered a print two foot high and put it on the mantelpiece.

Adam at 4 Sealy Road, Torbay, around 1974. The hair was getting pretty long, but it still had a way to go.

Robin and Adam at 4 Sealy Road, Torbay, around 1980.

Robin Dudding farewelling friends about to leave Lyttelton on the *Suevic*, around 1973. 'At some stage,' Bill Manhire said two decades later, 'someone will have to sit down and try to work out just what [Robin's] presence consists of, apart from the considerable beard.'

The Duddings on holiday on Great Barrier Island, January 1983. Back row (from left): Lois, Robin, Rachel's boyfriend John, Anna, Ruth, Ruth's boyfriend Ron. Middle: Melissa, Natasha. Front: Rachel, Adam, Melissa's boyfriend Brett.

Sealy Road, 1979: Robin plays ping-pong on the rain-warped table-tennis table, Natasha hangs out washing, and Woodspring Cottage, birthplace of *Mate* (nos 7–14) and *Islands* (nos 7–26), quietly rots. Photograph by Paul Buckley.

Robin Dudding, publisher and editor, as photographed by Glenn Jowitt for *Metro* magazine in 1984, around the time *Islands* was being resurrected after a three-year disappearance.

Robin and Lois Dudding at Sealy Road, around 2005.

parked in the wrong car park; the time Robin made mention of Donovan's ex-friend and sworn enemy Denis Glover during an address to the Library Association and Donovan spent the following week abusing him for having done so.

In early 1972 *Landfall* was once again dangerously close to missing its deadline, in part because space was being held for a particularly exciting piece of work – a complete, unpublished Katherine Mansfield short story from 1915, recently discovered by a Turnbull Library researcher.

Fed up, possibly a bit drunk, Donovan called Robin into his office to yell at him for a bit, but Robin grew tired of the abuse and walked out. The next day Donovan hauled him back in for some more, but this time he was really angry. 'You set me up,' he ranted. 'I'm managing director but you think you're superior to me, telling me what to do by walking out . . .' And he fired him.

For the following six weeks the pair wheeled about in a weird half-embrace, half-playground scrap, all conducted through letters.

At first both seemed interested in reversing the impetuous dismissal, but only if the other man would admit it was entirely his fault. Fat chance.

Then they discussed compromises – perhaps Robin could buy the *Landfall* name off Caxton or edit the magazine off-site on contract – but they couldn't agree on how to talk about these plans: Donovan wanted to discuss them over a few drinks and Robin didn't, so they never met.

Letters went back and forth. Donovan accused Robin of stealing *Landfall* files; Robin said he'd simply removed some personal correspondence because he feared Donovan was such a brute he'd misuse the sensitive material therein (such as a letter from Writer A slagging off his friend, Writer B, behind his back).

Donovan accused Robin of sabotaging *Landfall* by returning contributors' submissions after he was fired; Robin said that editing is a personal relationship not a corporate one so it would have been unethical not to give writers the opportunity to decide whether to resubmit once they knew who the new editor was, and *anyway* the real saboteur was *you* Mr Donovan when you cruelly fired me with one hour's notice.

Many of the Caxton staff were loyal to Robin. There were discussions about a possible walkout in his support, and he received regular covert updates about what Donovan was doing and saying.

Dad seemed as mystified as anyone as to the underlying reasons for his dismissal. His preferred theories, as laid out in letters to friends, were that the whisky had finally driven Donovan insane or that Caxton's continuing financial struggles had reached a point where shedding staff – he wasn't the only person fired that year – was worth the trouble it would cause.

Eventually the pair stopped communicating altogether. Donovan reneged on a promise to pay out Dad's superannuation in full. The final Dudding *Landfall*, edition 101 featuring the never-before-seen Mansfield story, was printed – late, of course, though Dad insisted if it weren't for his dismissal the issue would have made its deadline.

Caxton part-owner Leo Bensemann picked up the pieces and produced a rather ragged June issue of *Landfall*, while Robin worked in an utter frenzy on his next project: launching a bigger, better, properly independent magazine that he would edit and publish alone. Brasch instantly abandoned *Landfall* ('it's nothing – less than a ghost – without you,' he told Dad) and threw his weight, both moral and financial, behind the new Dudding project.

Dad wrote to all his writer friends and asked them to find something special for the launch issue. All suggestions for a name for his new mag were welcome.

In mid-September Robin spent a pleasant day in Port Chalmers collecting mussels and cockles with Ralph Hotere, and he left with a nice new Hotere painting under his arm. He also visited the printer John McIndoe: he wanted to be sure his new baby was looking good as she came off the press.

Hotere had designed the cover. The central image was a jumble of letters built from repeated impressions of rubber stamps of the words ONE and ISLANDS. The inking was uneven and the stamps overlapped and rotated to form random words and non-words: ƎNO, ONFONF, NEON, ONI, NONE, ONIONI.

Inside there was poetry by Allen Curnow, Vincent O'Sullivan, Russell Haley and Bill Manhire and a prose poem 'elegy' by James K. Baxter. There were stories by Ian Wedde and Michael Henderson, essays by Charles Brasch and Denis Glover, reviews by C.K. Stead, James Bertram and Alan Roddick. It was a star-studded contents list, 'an overwhelming vote of confidence in Robin Dudding's editorship', as the Christchurch *Press* reviewer put it. (As far as I can tell, no reviewer thought to comment on the absence of women contributors.)

After the launch, Ralph sent Dad a letter of congratulations and confession. He thought he'd better let him know 'before some bright Maori academic bastard' noticed it first, that there was a dirty joke lurking in the cover's apparently random typography: 'ONIONI' is Māori for the verb to wriggle the hips indecently, to copulate. It was, 'of course completely unintended!' wrote Ralph, lying through his teeth.

Brasch was supporting the magazine, but to feed the family Dad once again signed up for relief teaching, as well as labouring in people's gardens for $1.50 an hour and looking for freelance editing.

He also won occasional cash prizes by showing his chickens at agricultural fairs, though the winnings didn't stretch terribly far: in 1972 he entered six chooks in the Oamaru Show, spending $2.50 on entry fees, $1.60 to send them by train and 32¢ on Vaseline to get their legs and combs shining. Returns: 15¢ for best Wyandotte cockerel and 9¢ for the second-best Sussex hen. 'Hooray, hooray,' as he put it in a letter to his parents.

He was also earning rent from Sealy Road, but that didn't go terribly well either. One early tenant, a rather strange lawnmower man called Mr Dudley, fell half a year behind with the rent before Dad finally summoned the nerve to evict him from afar. For years afterwards they exchanged letters – Dad would write demanding Mr Dudley pay the $89.40 he owed, and Mr Dudley would reply with an envelope containing a couple of coins and a barely legible cover note: 'Mr Dudding. $87.40 to go not $89.40. enclosed is $0.40. leaves $87.' (About 15 years later, Dad and I were driving somewhere in Torbay when he pointed to a hunched figure of a man creeping along a footpath carrying a small petrol lawnmower on his back. 'That guy owes me $100,' he said.)

He was racing to get the next *Islands* out. Life was hectic. And yet, he said in a letter to writer Kevin Cunningham, just being free of the paranoiac, smog-bound atmosphere of Caxton meant he had 'a little more time to talk, relax, jump with the kids – go to [the hippy musical] Hair, look at sandhills, stroke my geese, wife etc . . .'

He bought a puppy called Emma. He started growing a beard. Even his moaning to Kevin was more upbeat than it had been in years:

> I was a fool of course to think I could toss off ISLANDS in between jobs, books, fucks . . . what have you. It's proving a very big job but I'm very determined to keep it going [. . .] For the present we stay in Chch with chooks, goose, dog, kids, half-acre and tumble-down Woodspring Cottage but eventually I hope we can move back to warmth and humidity and a place to grow tree tomatoes, oranges, bananas etc & pawpaw & peppers of course . . .

Less than a year later, Brasch died of cancer aged 63. Dad was bereft. He'd been due in Dunedin the following week and had kidded himself that Charles, who'd been ill for many months, was on the mend, that he would see him one last time.

'I'm faced with a huge loss,' he wrote to Kevin. 'It's not a very good admission but as I work on *Islands* I have this recurring thought – Charles isn't here to see it now.'

Islands was humming along, sustained by good reviews, growing circulation, Literary Fund grants and Brasch's backing, which continued for a while after his death via a bequest. But with Brasch gone, reasons for staying in the

South Island were running out. By the end of 1973 the decision was made: we were returning to Auckland.

Dad wound up his gardening and teaching jobs. Sold Barnes Road to the council for development as pensioner flats (the death-knell for my weeping gum, which was now 25 feet high). Dropped the geese off at a farm in Port Chalmers. Bought a near-new baby-blue Ford Transit and took me along to pick it up from the garage where workmen had installed a gas cooker and a fold-down bed. Squeezed in a family of eight and a dog and our worldly goods and started driving north, visiting everywhere on the way.

Brasch's mortgage on our Christchurch house was written off when he died, and the sale of the Christchurch house in a buoyant property market left enough change that Dad could sink a few thousand dollars into *Islands* and still have plenty of change for the van and then some. For the first time ever, the family finances were in surplus.

In the face of so few troubles, Dad needed a creative way to make his life difficult again. He packed a typewriter and his files into the Transit and attempted to edit *Islands* 7 on the road, over the six summery weeks of our migration back to Auckland.

The editing went terribly, but otherwise, I'm told, it was a hell of a trip. It seems a shame that the only part I remember is freaking out on that krill-covered beach in Nelson.

12. Three very short stories about Sealy Road

Chickens

Dad breeds the chickens and feeds the chickens, powders the chickens for lice and grooms the chickens for shows, and when it's time to eat one he cuts off its head with an axe and hangs it from the washing line on a piece of string tied around its feet.

The gutting, plucking and cooking are Mum's jobs. She hacks off the feet and hauls out the metallic-smelling viscera by the handful, working on a table in the garden to keep the flies out of the house.

She calls Anna and me over for an autopsy. We inspect the slimy coils of intestine, the cute little heart that isn't actually heart-shaped after all, the spongy pieces of lung that cling to the insides of the ribcage and have to be scraped out with your fingers.

'Look at this,' Mum says, bisecting the hard, rubbery gizzard with a sharp knife and showing us the gritty mess inside. 'She's been eating little stones to grind her corn.'

We take a chicken foot each and use our fingernails to grasp the slippery ends of the tendons, and pull them to make each claw clench and release, a final sign of life from the old bird.

Cigarettes

DAD BUYS his cigarettes in the smaller pack, 10 Pall Mall plain, because he's quitting tomorrow and anyway he's short of cash this week. Occasionally he gives me the money and I walk to the Torbay dairy to buy them and pick up a few milk bottles or pink smokers with the change, but usually he just stops the van and ducks in on the way back from a swim at Long Bay.

When I'm four, Dad and Rachel are proofreading galleys at the dining table (. . . *new line-quote-grandpa-question-unquote-new line-quote-not-him-comma-don't be stupid-stop* . . .) and he doesn't have an ashtray. He doesn't want to interrupt the flow, so he gives me the still-glowing butt to take to the compost bucket in the kitchen. I carry it off like a jewel, but once out of sight I test it. The bitter tang of the soggy strands of tobacco on my tongue is disgusting and the tiny suck of smoke is even worse. I drop it quickly into the compost bucket, where it hisses out in the soup of tea leaves and orange peel and feijoa skins.

He is forever complaining about not being able to quit smoking. Once, when he's taking his afternoon nap, I take a near-new pack of cigarettes from his office to the bathroom.

With the water running I tear each cigarette to pieces into the sink and swill it around until every shred of tobacco and paper has gone down the plughole. When he wakes up I tell him what I've done, and am offended when he doesn't thank me.

Flying

I'M STANDING in the small concrete courtyard by the front door at 4 Sealy Road, Torbay, Auckland 10, New Zealand, Earth, the Milky Way, with my arms extended, slowly turning round and round.

After a while I start tilting off-centre as I spin, like a spinning top just after it loses its balance, with my upper body describing ever-wider circles. Then I realise my feet have lifted slightly off the ground and I'm very slowly rising, spiralling up until I'm high enough to look down on the roof. I then waste much of the flight arguing with myself about whether this is a dream or not – I'm sure flying is impossible, and yet here I am, flying.

I have this dream all the time when I'm little, but as I get older years pass between recurrences. Every time I find myself flying above Sealy Road I know I've done this before, but then I struggle to work out whether that's because I can actually fly, or because I've dreamt about it before. After I wake up I lie there for ages, still not quite sure.

13. Four thousand holes in Blackburn, Lancashire

WITH HELP from my sisters I've compiled a list of the music that filled our house at Sealy Road when we were kids. I've turned it into a playlist to stream through my computer as I write the next few chapters.

> ... *Rubber Soul, Abbey Road* and *Sgt. Peppers.* Simon and Garfunkel's *Parsley, Sage, Rosemary and Thyme.* Schubert's tinkling Trout Quintet, which Mum would turn up really loud when she did the housework ...

It's a suggestion I heard in a memoir-writing workshop: look at photos, listen to the soundtrack of a particular time, trick your brain into unlocking some old memories.

> ... Harry Belafonte at Carnegie Hall with Miriam

Makeba and Odetta, Bob Dylan's *Greatest Hits*, the *Easy Rider* soundtrack, *Breakfast in America* . . .

Even before I hit play, the album names alone get me halfway there. I can vividly see the big square booklet of lyrics and trippy artwork that came with the multi-disc *Tommy* box set, and the lyrics on the back of the *Sgt. Pepper's Lonely Hearts Club Band* sleeve, with mysterious stories about holes in Blackburn, Lancashire printed in black type on red. I can hear Dad's rich tenor voice, not so much out of tune as using entirely different notes, singing along to Belafonte and Odetta's epic, hilarious version of 'A Hole in the Bucket'.

. . . *The Gondoliers*, the Animals, *Great Opera Choruses* including the one where everyone bashes on anvils in time, *Jesus Christ Superstar*, the *West Side Story* soundtrack . . .

I line up 20 or so albums and hit play. It's like getting in a time machine. I'm sucked back to the living room in Sealy Road, to the scratchy red-and-brown woollen throw on the couch, to the big chipboard record-player cabinet with its built-in speaker behind a cloth grille, and space for records inside. I listen to the *Hair* soundtrack from start to finish, enthralled, unsure why my eyes keep filling. *Tommy*, though, is much more dreadful than I remember it.

I twiddle the time machine dial – forwards to Supertramp's *Breakfast in America* (bought by a sister in 1979); backwards to a Simon and Garfunkel album that was being belted out long before I was born. Forward again to, say, 7 o'clock on a Saturday morning in the mid-70s, at the precise moment that Dad drops the stylus onto the edge of a spinning LP, and there are a few seconds of loud crackle then the three soft opening chords of Tchaikovsky's 1812 Overture; 12 minutes later the cannons start firing, rattling the windows and bringing half a dozen children complaining from their beds.

We left the beer bottles in Christchurch but not the wooden planks, and once he'd collected enough new DB empties, Dad rebuilt his bookshelves in Torbay. Eventually, inevitably, a visiting toddler climbed a shelf and brought planks, bottles and books tumbling down, so Dad built pine shelves onto three of the living-room walls, floor to ceiling, apart from a space for the piano and another for a sofa. One light switch ended up inside a shelf, so a wooden spoon was left nearby where you could use it to prod the switch without having to remove half a dozen books.

Children's books were within arm's reach above the sofa. Big art books were at floor level. Along a topmost shelf was a really old edition of the complete Charles Dickens, with faded red covers and gold lettering. Penguin, Puffin and Pelican paperbacks had an aviary of their own. Poetry was here, New Zealand non-fiction there, a long row of *Landfall*s and *Island*s over there.

The books shared the shelves with dust, fly spray cans, dead flies, apple cores, coffee mugs and a number of miniature plastic, china and wooden chickens, which was all anyone could ever think of as a Christmas present for Dad.

I'd often lie in a state of foggy-headed sloth on the sofa, rereading picture books I'd read hundreds of times before, mainly because that's what I could reach without having to stand up. But most of the thousands of books lining the wall were just background, a wallpaper that I'd scan idly while pushing my lamb's fry, mashed potato and silverbeet around my dinner plate: the complete Walter de la Mare, the collected Auden, *The Pocket Mirror* by Janet Frame, an edition of Joyce's *Ulysses* with an archer's bow drawn on its spine.

I was especially intrigued by a book on the top shelf: *Giles Goat-Boy* by John Barth, which had a black shiny spine and a red, eyeless goat-devil mask printed above the title. It never occurred to me to actually take the book down and read it.

Some days it seemed reading was the only thing happening at Sealy Road. Older sisters in the garden sunbathing with a fat book or studying for exams. Mum sitting on the front doorstep with a cup of tea and a Maigret mystery. Dad reading contributors' bad poetry in Woodspring Cottage. (His garden-shed study had inherited the plaque pilfered from Barnes Road.) Anna reading something terrible like *Flowers in the Attic*. Me reading or rereading *James and the Giant Peach*, Enid Blyton, *Narnia*, the continuing adventures of Professor Branestawm, or a James Thurber collection Dad had just finished reading, even though the adult point of the cartoons went over my head.

Later I'd work my way, keen but bogged down by the dense sentences, through *Sherlock Holmes* and H. G. Wells, Jane Austen and Edgar Allen Poe. Occasionally I'd set myself a school-holiday goal of reading a top-shelf Dickens, butter-knife at hand to slice open the uncut pages. There was pleasure in the snicking slice itself, and in the knowledge that these pages had never before been read, but I didn't always make it to the end.

I was six when my sister Ruth read out the bit in *Gulliver's Travels* where Gulliver, untied by the Lilliputians, empties his bladder in a torrent of piss that astonishes the little people with its noise and violence. Impressed by the author's naughtiness, I struggled through the whole thing, pulled in deep by the exciting or funny bits, but bobbing back up to the surface each time I hit a stretch of baffling words or concepts. The word wasn't pronounced 'dome sticks', Mum explained, looking over my shoulder. The accent was on the middle syllable, and it was an old-fashioned word for servants, spelt with an extra K.

Dad took us to the library, bought us new books on birthdays, and sometimes pulled out something from our own shelves, such as Alastair Airey's 1960 book *The Boys of Puhawai*, set in a fictionalised North Island community and featuring actual Māori characters, which Dad figured would add a bit of roughage to our mostly British reading diet.

When I was five and Anna was eight Dad asked us to help him with something. Did we want to be a test audience for the manuscript of a children's story by his friend Maurice Gee?

Night after night we squashed into an armchair with Dad as he read us the next chapter of 'The Smiths and the Joneses', a brilliant, terrifying story about giant shapeshifting slug creatures who arrived in Auckland and planned to turn the planet into a grey sludge unless redhead twins called Rachel and Theo and an old man called Mr Jones could stop them.

We were gripped, and the older sisters often listened in too. I can still see the images the story evoked and remember the queasiness of imagining slime-filled tunnels beneath our feet linking the city's volcanos. Anna told Dad she was pleased to have finally found a story in which characters went to the toilet, something whose absence bothered her in other fiction. By the time the book was published in early 1979, Gee had changed the baddies' names from the Smiths to the

Wilberforces and the book's title to *Under the Mountain*.

What I didn't realise until I was reading letters in the Turnbull Library was that, despite Anna's and my endorsement and his own huge admiration of Gee's writing, Dad hated the book. He wrote to Gee, quoting something Carson McCullers' editor had once written to her: 'I must insist that a story should have a reason for being. Must rise, make a point, that is inside the tale itself, and at the same time outside in the world.'

'The Smiths and the Joneses', said Dad, for all its storytelling competence, didn't have that reason for being. It was 'grey, slimy, nasty [. . .] Excrescence rather than inspiration; effective local colour but attached to nought.

'Obviously, Moss, I don't need to write this as you need not take any notice, but I'd feel a little culpable if I didn't say what I think. Every good writer has to write a bummer [. . .] I think this is your bummer – I think you should sweep it under the bed. Sorry.'

Luckily for Moss he didn't sweep it under the bed. *Under the Mountain* became one of his most successful books, and was adapted for TV and then a feature film. When I got my own hardback copy the year it came out I read it another half-dozen times. Anna and I were still obsessed with the story a year later. In another letter to Gee, Dad said he'd taken us for walk on Mt Eden's volcanic cone and we had 'recited Jones-type incantations before galloping down the crater'.

When I went to interview Maurice Gee, I told him how I'd been boasting to friends for decades that I had heard *Under the Mountain* before just about anyone else in the country. Maurice was glad I liked it, but said he didn't even remember having sent Dad the manuscript.

I was on holiday with Mum at her parents' place in Pukekohe one summer when I found a copy of John Irving's *The World According to Garp* for $1 in a second-hand bookshop. I knew Dad had read it and had laughed out loud several times, which seemed a good recommendation. He might even have read out a few pages.

By the time we got home I was a third of the way through it and hooked, but Dad made me hand it over, confiscated. I was 11 – far too young to read it.

Even now, I'm not quite sure why. Certainly *Garp* has some adult moments – it opens with a dying man being milked of his sperm by a nurse who wants a fatherless child, and later features a horrifying blowjob-plus-car crash scene, as well as a band of psychotic feminists who cut out their tongues in solidarity with a rape victim who'd suffered the same.

Yet Dad hadn't censored my reading before this. It seemed particularly unfair because despite *Garp*'s preoccupation with sex, it was actually Irving's big characters and romping storylines I was loving – the rude bits were just a bonus. And anyway, books far worse than *Garp* were on our own bookshelves if you could be bothered looking, and I'd reached the age where I could be bothered. I'd become adept at skimming Harold Robbins and Jackie Collins novels for the best bits, or in the case of books borrowed from likeminded friends, lightly cradling a book in my hands to see which pages it fell open at.

Unlike some of my friends' houses, Sealy Road had no paternal cache of *Playboy* or *Penthouse*, but on the bottom shelf in the living room, alongside the huge hardback of the art of Leonardo Da Vinci, you could find Alex Comfort's *The Joy of Sex*, whose explicit drawings were fine as long as you averted your eyes from the bearded man. On the shelf near the fireplace were hundreds of tatty fiction paperbacks, and there was some gold in there: John Cleland's outrageous 1748 novel *Fanny Hill*, which didn't even require skimming as every page was pure filth; *Lolita* (though this had a disproportionate amount of boring literature around the brief rude bits); Roald Dahl's mildly kinky adult books *Kiss Kiss* and *Switch Bitch*. On the shelf above the piano, next to a set of Anaïs Nin's diaries, was a copy of Nin's *Delta of Venus*, a series of elegantly sordid erotic vignettes produced on demand for a pervy Parisian businessman in the 1940s. Apparently he was always complaining to Nin that the stories contained too much poetry and not enough action.

Long before my furtive prowling of the shelves for the perversions of Nin or Nabokov I had learnt the un-titillating facts of life from a big coffee-table book that I presume Mum or Dad had bought for just that purpose, called *Birth, Conception and Contraception*. It had a drawing of an upside-down baby in utero on the cover and inside were big beautiful drawings of a foetus progressing from a ball of cells to a strange seahorse creature to a ready-to-be-born baby. The pictures of penises and vaginas were more scientific than erotic, especially the mystifying cutaway diagrams; the one showing the position of the ovaries and fallopian tubes in a woman's belly looked like the woman had eaten the handlebars of a Raleigh Chopper.

In any case, I knew what naked people looked like. Both my parents seemed to consider clothes as useful things for keeping warm but not much else, so if the weather was clement and there weren't any visitors to shock they wore little or nothing around the house. Dad liked to be naked in the sun especially, though when gardening he'd usually make concessions to safety and sunburn and put on some underpants and a hat.

The shock of the Duddings' return to Auckland was softened by our discovery of a band of new soulmates living just around the corner. The Delaneys – Carol and Mick and their four daughters – had arrived from England a few months earlier. Their girls were classmates of ours, and when our families met en masse we became a single tribe that happened to have two houses, four parents and 10 children. Whichever house you found yourself in at mealtimes or bedtimes, that's where you'd eat or sleep, possibly on a mattress on the floor. As recent escapees from Christchurch and Leicester respectively, the Duddings and Delaneys couldn't get enough of Auckland beaches. We spent a lot of time at Long Bay.

It was a brief, almost euphoric, family love affair, but within a year the Delaneys realised the move to New Zealand had been a financial disaster and they fled back to the UK (though they returned for good some years later).

Even without them, there was a steady stream of visitors at Sealy Road: young writers like Michael Morrissey paying court at the editor's house, or longstanding literary friends like the Manhires or the Weddes or the Stoneses visiting for lunch and a beach walk. School friends and neighbouring kids wandered in and out. John Murray from next door would pop over after dinner for a game of crib or ping-pong. The talk might be of books and art and politics, but more important was the latest ping-pong score, or the fluffy newly hatched chicks Dad would bring up from the fowl-run to show off.

When I was seven I brought home an entry form for a colouring competition run by the local supermarket – a cartoonish outline of a clown with giant shoes, curly wig and oversized overalls. On Saturday after lunch, as a gaggle of visitors mopped up the last of their soup with a slice of Mum's bread, I found my felt-tip pens and started planning a prize-winning colouring-in effort. I was finding it a struggle, perhaps because of a lack of experience – Mum followed the Playcentre mantra that colouring between the lines of a pre-drawn picture corroded a child's natural artistic expression and probably verged on child abuse.

I asked for help, and seeing one of the visitors was Ralph Hotere, Dad suggested he help me – Ralph was a real artist, after all. Hotere's advice, predictably enough, was that I should set aside the obvious pink, red, yellow and orange and see what I could achieve with the black felt-tip alone. How about lots of black dots all over the clown's overalls?

I did as he suggested, but even before I'd started dabbing away at the clown I knew in my heart that a giant mess of black blotches wasn't what the lady at the supermarket would be looking for when she judged the competition. By the time I'd finished it looked terrible and I was in despair. After Ralph left, I screwed it up, threw it in the bin and raged and stamped a little.

After seven years away from Auckland, my parents were appalled by the changes they saw when we returned. Motorways were pushing ever further north and developers were subdividing the North Shore to death, bulldozing monstrous yellow scars into the hills then carpeting them with gigantic $60,000 houses, whose owners had to buy topsoil to cover the clay and work night and day to pay their huge mortgages.

Still, Dad told Kevin in a 1974 letter, he was enjoying the city's hills after Christchurch's flatness, and there were things that made the return more than worthwhile: 'Peace at night from traffic silent, quiet changing beaches, warmth of the shorts & barefoot variety, drumming rain.'

He planted plum, peach, apple and lemon, but Auckland's swelter could also support Ecuadorian babaco, Chinese loquat, South American tamarillo, passionfruit, banana passionfruit, grape, banana. His garden was a seed bank and a history lesson – capsicums from a strain bred by Frank Sargeson; flower bulbs and tomato seeds from his parents' garden in Hawke's Bay; a kauri sapling, planted as a kind of successor to my ill-fated Barnes Road weeping gum, which I had to stand in front of on every birthday, so Dad could take a photo showing which was winning the skyward race, tree or boy.

No geese in Auckland, but many chooks, occasionally ducks and, once, pheasants. Just the one dog, Emma, but a succession of cats. Briefly, piteously, a lamb called Tess, whom we'd feed warm formula from a beer bottle with a rubbery nipple on its end, as her tail whipped like a helicopter blade. Dad named her after Thomas Hardy's tragic heroine, which may have sealed her fate: when she was a year old, Tess was dropped back at her birth-farm to give Dad a week to fence off the fruit trees she'd been hungrily ringbarking, but at the farm she chewed a freshly tanalised fencepost and died horribly of arsenic poisoning.

There were two beaches we considered our own. Waiake we walked to, towels around necks, a Frisbee or softball passing between us. The beach was small, sheltered and often waveless, a place to get sunburnt, swim out to the raft, prod rock-pool anemones to watch them snap close, climb the pōhutukawa, stand in the shallows throwing something around. In 1975 friends who'd moved to Iowa sent us a taste of the American consumer dream – a real Frisbee-brand 'Moonlighter' that not only flew further and flatter than anything you could get in New Zealand, but also *glowed in the dark*. As dusk fell we'd keep throwing the Moonlighter around as a matter of principle, even after it had become impossible to judge the distance to the ghostly greenish-white disc as it loomed suddenly out of the darkness and hit you in the face.

Long Bay we drove to, Dad at the wheel, Mum in the passenger seat, the rest of us and the dog rolling around on the fold-down bed in the back of the Transit, along with the polystyrene surfboards that left a rash on your stomach. Long Bay was the place for long walks with kids running rings around the conversing adults, for beach cricket, for serious bodysurfing if the wind had been blowing in the right direction, for collecting pipi and tuatua that you could take home and make into sand-gritty fritters or steam open on a beach barbecue in some beer and butter.

For several years Dad invited the 30-odd families in our street to a Long Bay January barbecue. One year, he decided to use a bottle of methylated spirits to encourage a reluctant barbecue. I was five metres away, but a gust of wind caught the stream of meths and a line of flame shot across the grass between us, and suddenly my feet were engulfed in flickering blue flames and everyone was screaming. The flames burnt so coolly that I was unharmed, but Dad never really got the hang of flammable liquids. A couple of decades later he burnt off an eyebrow and two-thirds of his beard after using petrol to restart a rubbish fire in the garden.

The motorways and developers kept pushing north. New hills were scraped back to clay and existing sections were sliced into halves and quarters to squeeze in ever-bigger houses, leaving no room for a garden you could feed a family from, or a respectable fowl-run. Dad despaired of it all. But just because he hated motorways didn't mean he couldn't enjoy them.

In 1979, when the northern motorway was stretched an extra 3km north to reach Sunset Road, Dad loaded everyone into the Transit and led us on a semi-legal stroll along the virgin tarmac a few days before it was opened to vehicles. We booted a soccer ball along the median strip, turned cartwheels in the passing lane and had competitions to see who could throw a Frisbee over the overbridges. When Dad spotted a mountain of roading gravel on the roadside he dared us to run up it, and we ended up rolling around, our pockets filling with stones. When we got back to the van he couldn't find his keys. We went back to the gravel mountain to look for them but it was hopeless, and it was getting dark. We finally got home in two taxis Dad couldn't really afford.

Eventually the motorway went all the way to Torbay and far beyond. When he was driving home from the city, Dad would come off it a few exits early and head east to the winding coast road, so that when he reached the crest of the hill between Browns Bay and Torbay he could once again catch that first sight of the waters of Waiake, with Whangaparāoa Peninsula far in the distance, and say in a voice of wonderment, 'Ah the sea, the sea . . .'

Mum has dug out a box of her old letters for me to have a look at. They are sorted by correspondent into a couple of dozen large brown envelopes. One envelope, though, is different. It's labelled 'UNSENT', and contains half a dozen letters Mum wrote but never got round to posting.

Their dates range from 1975 to 1982. Some, I suspect, were just mislaid after writing, and by the time they turned up again they were too old to bother sending. A couple date from the time when money was so horribly tight that she quite possibly couldn't afford a stamp. But there is one, an elegantly stroppy letter to the deputy principal of my primary school, which I think she wrote as an act of catharsis then didn't dare post.

One of reasons I've decided to write a book about Dad is that he was unusual. Yet, the more I look back at their lives, the more I realise it's actually Mum who was the more deeply unconventional of the pair.

The two pages of this unsent letter contain so much of Mum's character – the way she used to burble on and take forever to make a point, her disapproval of authority and systems, her gentle yet serious *unusualness* – that I asked her if I could reproduce it, and she said, 'Sure. Why not?'

4 Sealy Road
Torbay
1st July '76

Dear Mrs. Baird,

This is to acknowledge receipt of your cyclostyled letter telling me that Anna and Adam were late on June 28th (Monday of this week.)

You were probably quite right to bring it to my doorstep,

so to speak, as indeed I am the one responsible for getting up and shaking the children awake on dark wintry mornings and hustling them out the door whether it's sunny or rainy or snowy; and what's more I admit that quite apart from winter's deterrent to leaping out early, I am a chronic latecomer – no matter how soon I start getting ready. In that sense responsibility is fairly and squarely mine. On the other hand I'm not much use, for I've been aware of this problem for 36 years and no amount of detention, lines, embarrassment or abuse have helped me be on time. I've noticed that one of my children, now adult, is like me here. We're good spellers, have a flair for language but we always run for buses. Another daughter shines at mathematics and music – she's never late. A third – a good half-miler – is always early. But then one day she completely missed her ride because she stayed back helping along a friend with a twisted ankle. And so on. Personalities vary – circumstances change things. Then again from the point of view of stages:– at some time all of my children have shown great reluctance to go to school and I have tried every means of persuasion and coercion to get them there. It seems to be usually in the first couple of years of starting. I find they eventually get over their antipathy (or do they resign themselves to the unchangeable?) and get on with it. Homes are not perfect and of course schools aren't and if we fussed over every factor we would despair. As an example – Adam has had 4 new teachers and 3 new classrooms in 5 months this year (5 teachers since starting 8 months ago.) I think you will agree that coping with so many changes in so short a time is a lot to expect of any 5 year old. We're very lucky that he likes school as much as he undoubtedly does.

Since, as far as I know, these two children are not giving

you problems in academic, social or classroom-behaviour spheres, I can only guess that their lateness is looked at from a school tidiness and disciplinary point of view. I'm pretty confident that they will be responsible, caring and law-abiding adults despite their tardiness. No less than Will Shakespeare noted the picture of the schoolboy "creeping like snail unwillingly to school". That stage led, before you knew it, to the learned judge, staid and boring no doubt.

Still, I sympathise with you standing out there at the gate on that bleak, windy Glamorgan Drive and I don't want the kids getting anxious about this matter so I'll try to shuffle them along a little sooner.

Thank you for the letter – it set me thinking, but don't waste postage for I'll probably be up at the school each week at sports time.

Yours faithfully
Lois Dudding.

Mum's anti-establishment views weren't always filed away unsent. A few years later, when my sister's high school was on the brink of introducing a new uniform, both parents went to the public meeting to express their concern, but Mum decided that the best way to demonstrate that *all* school uniforms – old or new – were demeaning, unflattering and depressingly conformist was to turn up to the meeting squeezed into a schoolgirl's uniform herself. I imagine it had an impact, but probably not the one she had in mind.

If you'd asked me before I was 10 what I thought of my Dad I'd have said he was the best dad around. He was a bit like how you might imagine God: strong, potentially scary when wrathful but usually kind and gentle, there when you needed him, patient, wise, omniscient, big beard. I guess a lot of boys think much the same before they're 10.

Mum was more obviously brainy than him. She was the one who knew facts and used big words and who would read for fun a book about lateral thinking or the evolution of invertebrates, but we knew it was Dad who set the rules, made all the big decisions, drove the van, controlled the money, bought the Christmas presents, planned the outings, made the final call on what time you had to be home.

If Mum asked me to do the dishes or sweep the floor I'd ignore her, figuring if she seriously wanted it done she'd ask me three more times and then lose her temper, at which point I'd do it grudgingly and badly. If Dad told me to collect the eggs or mow the lawn I did it right away, because disobeying didn't seem an option, even though I couldn't have said what the consequence might be. When a friend told me his parents hit him with a wooden spoon if he was bad I thought he was pulling my leg. I thought corporal punishment was something that only happened in books by Roald Dahl.

Less godlike were Dad's habits of popping out his upper false teeth during dinner when I had school friends over, and of walking into a room, lifting his leg 20 degrees sideways and unleashing a lengthy, theatrically noisy fart followed by a smug grin. I was embarrassed when he got me to help him trawl nearby streets in his van during the annual inorganic rubbish collections, in search of chicken-wire, timber or roof iron for his never-ending project of building and repairing fowl-houses.

We did a lot together. Morning swims at Waiake. Evening

runs at Long Bay. I'd help him in the garden (boring and arduous), cleaning out the fowl-houses (boring and smelly), and proofreading *Islands* – which could have been boring except that by the time I was eight he was paying me $4 an hour to do so and I was getting good enough to pick up on the deliberate mistakes he'd make to test me, like replacing the word 'sheep' with 'goat'. As I got older and started seeing girls differently, I noticed that if we drove past a pretty girl on a bus stop Dad would be distracted in the same way as I was, which I found both embarrassing and revolting. Some things aren't meant to be shared.

He sometimes called me 'Addie', and also 'love' or 'luvvie', which was fine as long as we weren't in public. He used to drive me nuts by sometimes saying 'good girl' instead of 'good boy' when praising me, presumably because that's what he'd been saying to his five daughters for two decades. Mum married him in 1958 because she thought he'd make a good father, and she was right.

The letters I've been reading show Dad's professional life during this period was built, as ever, on a foundation of anxiety and near-panic, but even he was able to see that things were actually going pretty well. *Islands* was a success, even if the miraculous day when it covered its own costs hadn't quite arrived, and even though the slow slippage between intended and actual publication dates had already begun. He never stopped complaining to friends like Kevin Ireland about the guilt of failing to balance fatherhood with his work, his garden, his chooks, his leaking roof, yet in reality he spent more time with his kids than many fathers. His balancing act was actually pretty good – as long as he didn't look down.

There's a series of letters he wrote to Mum in early 1975, when she was in Wellington on her own for a week and he was managing the movements of six children aged 4 to 16 while trying, and mainly failing, to get out to his shed to work. His letters recount, day by day, the busy, messy, joyous shambles of 4 Sealy Road.

He tries to drop Adam at Playcentre, but has to cadge a ride from our neighbour Wendy because the van has a flat tyre. He gets a letter from a *Listener* reporter who wants to interview him about literary magazines. He sends Natasha, 10, up to the shops to buy a pack of fags, watches a tui sitting on the lancewood in the garden, buys Rachel, 16, a bra, and pops over to Wendy's with Melissa, 12, for half an hour of cards with Wendy's husband Roger. He enforces the older girls' meal-cooking roster, reads the kids *Watership Down* and *Nurse Matilda* at bedtime, and sleeps badly because the full moon is shining through the window. The next morning he has another flat tyre so Wendy gives him another lift.

There are visitors: Dot from next door seeking respite from her kids, followed minutes later by her kids; the husband of Ruth's violin teacher, who wants to talk about a violin; Michael Morrissey wants to talk about a story he's written; a school mum pops in in search of her child and is so impressed by the huge photo on the mantelpiece of naked Lois breastfeeding that she gets her own breasts out to show Dad how they're not as good as Lois's (she's as 'mad as a two-bob watch', as Dad observes).

He takes Adam and Jeremy (Wendy's four-year-old son) to the city on the Devonport ferry and they take the lift to the 19th floor of the Air New Zealand skyscraper. He oversees a Sunday night party organised by Rachel, 16, and Ruth, 14.

Rachel says he's welcome to stay around for the party, because he's been 'neat'. The girls' drama teacher Mr Stevens turns up with his young family, so at 9 o'clock his three kids are asleep in Dad's bed, Anna and Adam are in their own beds and Natasha and Melissa have decamped with sleeping bags to Wendy's. At 1 in the morning Dad is trying to fix a departing partygoer's flat battery and at 2 he gives up and drops them home.

There are more visitors: Mrs Flynn from round the corner looking for a Dudding girl to babysit her kids that evening; school friends of Ruth's looking for her; Tony Stones looking for a chat; Wendy again, at dinner time, with a casserole and baked potatoes for the whole family. In the afternoon an intense young woman Dad has never met before knocks on the door. She is from Hawke's Bay and they knew some families in common. More importantly, though, she had long admired *Islands* and is willing to work for him for nothing. She doesn't seem to want to leave but eventually he gets her out the door. 'These women,' Dad tells Mum, 'are driving me up the wall.'

14. The women

APRIL 2015. Mum and Carol and Mick Delaney are having lunch. Carol has served us each a vast slice of homemade quiche, my recorder is running in the middle of the table, and we're talking about the past: about how the Duddings and Delaneys and all their children hit it off so well back in 1974 when we'd just returned from Christchurch and they'd just arrived from Leicester. About the wonders of Long Bay Beach and the Waiwera hot pools. About how sad everyone was when the Delaneys disappeared back to England for half a decade when we'd only just got to know them. About Dad and Carol.

From the start, there was a network of interweaving links between the two families: Mick was especially fond of the youngest Dudding daughter, Anna; I trailed around like a puppy behind Sarah, three years old than me; my sister Natasha was best mates with Caz Delaney who was in the same year at school, and so on. But there was an especially close connection between Dad and Carol. When I asked Carol if I could visit her to talk about Dad, she said sure – but she suggested I bring

Lois along too and we'd make a lunch of it. So here we all are.

Carol is saying she and Dad would go for long walks together to Long Bay, usually with our dog Emma, sometimes with three-year-old me. They would talk about this and that, but especially about poetry. Carol had recently discovered the poetry of D. H. Lawrence, and she and Robin would stride the cliffs and shoreline discussing Lawrence's fragmentary 'pensées' of the 1920s, in which he condemned bourgeoisie and wage-slavery and dark satanic mills – just the sort of thing that resonated for Carol as a brainy, left-wing Londoner with working-class roots. She especially liked Lawrence's five-line poem 'Immorality', which she thought described the way people with depression treat those closest to them – people like her husband Mick, say, who's periodically been visited by the black dog all his life. The poem in full goes:

It is only immoral
to be dead-alive
sun-extinct
and busy putting out the sun
in other people.

Carol is talking about all this when Mick, a quiet, thoughtful, sweet guy who was a printer for most of his working life, clears his throat and says, 'Lois. Can I ask you a personal question?'

'Uhuh,' says Mum, through her quiche.

'In 1974, did you ever think Robin and Carol were having an affair?'

'No,' says Mum.

'You didn't?'

'No.'

'Well I did,' says Mick. 'That was one of the reasons, raking through my memory, that I thought we'd better get out of New Zealand, because it was all going wrong.'

'When?' says Mum, which isn't the question I'd have asked.

'1974,' says Mick. 'When Carol and Robin were out together a lot.'

'Yes,' says Mum. 'I knew they did.'

Group conversations are especially difficult for Mum to follow – the cross-conversations turn to fog – and I'm not sure how well she's keeping up, but I'm pretty sure she means she knew Carol and Robin spent a lot of time together, not that she knew about an affair. But now I'm confused too. I ask the obvious question.

'So *were* you having an affair?' I ask Carol.

'No,' says Carol. 'But it was a bit like an affair. There was a very strong bond, and there was a lot of attraction. Maybe in a different time and place you might, but we were part of a network, with all the children and so on. We didn't have an affair.'

I ask Mick: 'If you were so worried, did you ask Carol about it directly?'

'No,' says Mick.

'Oh you did,' Carol corrects him. 'On the plane when we left. You asked me on the plane.'

Carol was hardly the only woman to develop this kind of more-than-just-friends relationship with Dad. Some of them were there in the letters I saw in the Turnbull.

'I like you & love you and need you,' wrote one *Islands*

contributor who used to visit Sealy Road quite a bit. 'I am married, you are married, you can relate to me just fine on those terms, and it is my feelings which screw up, at least, a friendship.'

Another writer fretted: 'If I stopped to think about it, I'd never come near you again,' and added, in a postscript: 'I'm sleeping with gurus when it's offered.' (I'm not sure if this was a coy invitation, or a factual update about some other guru or gurus she had encountered.)

Another woman, a family friend for a time, wrote a touch wistfully, 'Dearest Robin, Since you left [. . .] it became clearer how much you meant to me . . .' Yet another woman wrote: 'In some strange way I still look to you for approval of the things I do and am. Is that healthy?'

Both Mum and my older sisters say it was always obvious to them that Dad was very keen, flirtatious even, with Wendy Galvin, the helpful (and beautiful) neighbouring mum who saved the day with rides to Playcentre and dropped-off casseroles. 'Though,' says Mum, 'I don't think he would have taken her to bed or anything.'

As with the Delaneys, the Galvin and Dudding families were interwoven. Our girls babysat their kids. Dinners and favours were exchanged. Before I started school I was best friends with the oldest son, Jeremy, a reckless, exciting kid who taught me how to ride a bike and led me on Red Indian-style sorties through the bush where we'd break branches, try to start a fire, or leave a poo amid the leaf litter. Jeremy's dad had a car that didn't break down and a job that wasn't conducted from a shed in his garden, and their house had unusual things: carpet, indoor toilets, central heating, a TV that Jeremy and I would lie in front of, feet waggling, to watch *Batman* and *The Six Million Dollar Man*.

But, just as with the Dudding–Delaney friendship, there was an especially strong connection between our Dad and their Mum. Wendy, 10 years Dad's junior, would come over and she and he would talk for ages in his office. Dad would drop in for a coffee at her place as he walked to the Torbay dairy for his 10 Pall Mall plain. When Wendy struggled to cope after the birth of her third child, Dad would bring the weeks-old baby back to our house for emergency feeds of mashed banana and yoghurt.

The Galvins moved away from Torbay in the mid-70s and the families lost touch, but I find Wendy in the phone book. When we meet she says she remembers the kindness of Lois and Robin and their support as she struggled, never an earth mother, with being stuck at home with young kids. She remembers her middle-class amazement at Lois's uncomplaining acceptance of the Sealy Road clutter and poverty, and the shitty little kitchen. When I ask if there'd been anything more to her relationship with Dad than standard neighbourly amity, she said no. But she also said she'd never noticed Dad was smitten with her, so I'm not quite sure what to make of that.

Anyway, after Carol and Mick Delaney and their four children escaped back to England the families kept in touch with exchanges of letters and photos, and Dad and Carol maintained a separate, more personal correspondence for a couple of years.

Looking at it now, says Carol, she can see what happened between Dad and her (and presumably between Dad and other women) as a kind of *emotional* infidelity. She recalls

Robin saying to her at the time that Lois had told him she felt a bit envious of the pleasure he was clearly getting out of this thing he had with Carol, whatever it was.

Mum nods.

'That was typical Lois,' says Carol. 'She put her finger on it.' But in those days, 'having an affair meant having a sexual relationship, so if you didn't have a sexual relationship you hadn't had an affair'.

We work away at the last of the quiche, and Carol and I speculate about what Dad might have thought he was doing. Carol wonders if Robin had some sort of emotional need that meant he felt he couldn't afford to expose himself to Lois.

I say that as long as he was able to get away with it, it was probably rather pleasant being a serial non-adulterer: he'd have got that fluttery feeling of first attraction and the establishment of something that's deeper than just flirting, but still bypassed the messiness of an 'affair'.

'Hmm,' says Carol. 'All the build-up but none of the repercussions. I could do with one of those.'

'Talking about affairs,' says Mick. 'I don't think people have affairs any more, do they? They just fuck.'

Mum laughs.

Perhaps this conversation should be awkward, but it really isn't. It's just three old friends, average age 79, plus the 44-year-old son of one of them, talking about a fourth old friend who's not there, and sifting through the embers, or ashes really, of long-ago loves and longings.

Mick talks about the relative promiscuity of different branches of his family tree (the Cockney lot were always 'carrying on' but the Irish Catholics on the other side never did), and Carol talks about her southeast London childhood, when her neighbours would head south to Kent for the summer hop-picking season – *dahn 'opping* – during which everyone lived in huts, turned brown as a berry in the sun, and the natural matrimonial laws were out the window for the duration. But eventually we return to Dad and his women.

'I suppose,' says Mum, 'that most wives wouldn't have stood for it.'

'I think that with Lois it was confidence,' says Carol. 'She knew Robin would never leave and what did it matter anyway, because she'd rather go and read her book than get wound up about something that wasn't worth it. She's a very secure woman.'

Perhaps, I suggest to Mum (in another of those complicated leading questions that make me worry I'm just putting words in her mouth but without which we'd never get anywhere), you did find these close friendships Dad had with other women uncomfortable or galling, but you thought it would be narrow-minded or old-fashioned for you to complain about them, whereas a more conventional woman who listened more to her gut than her brain would simply have known she didn't like it and ordered him to knock it off.

'Yes,' says Mum (which I hope means she agrees with the entire sentence). 'But some were stronger than others. Some friendships I didn't like so much. This particular girl I wasn't sure.'

I say: 'Do you mean the actual affair? The one in Christchurch?'

'Yes. But he got over it. It was not very long. It was before Anna was born.'

Mick speaks up again. 'Lois, I think you should prepare yourself for the disclosure that you were married to a serial womaniser.'

We all laugh, Mum loudest.

'You might have some more children somewhere,' says Carol. 'He liked begatting. That was one of his favourite things.'

As fascinating as it would be, I'm neither hoping nor expecting to uncover a long-lost half-sibling. A string of mistresses seems unlikely too, and I'm not quite up to the task of asking every woman Dad knew if there was anything dodgy about their friendship. But I need to know more about this Christchurch affair Mum has already told me about.

It was February when Mum first mentioned it. By the time we eat quiche with the Delaneys, it's April. I then put off hunting in earnest for the woman until July, and it's surprisingly slow going – I can't find her in the phone book or the electoral roll or on Facebook or in any of the other obvious places. Each time I hit a dead end I feel a mix of relief and irritation. I still feel uneasy about the entire sheet-sniffing, peeping-Tom exercise, but I also know I need to keep going till I find her.

I feel slightly less grubby when a friend points out that this is sometimes what happens when you write a book about a parent. Apparently when the Wellington academic Tim Beaglehole began researching a biography of his father J.C. Beaglehole in the 1990s he uncovered his father's long affair with a colleague and was so shocked he considered abandoning the biography. In the end he wrote it, including details of the affair, and pre-emptively defended himself in the introduction by noting that even such top-notch biographers as James Boswell and Lytton Strachey had understood the importance of scuttlebutt to a personal portrait. If it's good enough for Tim, James and Lytton, it's good enough for me.

Once I find the woman it's easy to see why it has taken so long. Since 1967 she's divorced, remarried and divorced, changed her surname three times and her first name once, left New Zealand, started a new professional career in middle age, retired and returned to a different New Zealand city. By early August I finally have her contact details and I email her to set up a phone interview. Her name is Kate.* She was the daughter of Dinny Donovan, the Caxton boss who sacked Dad in 1972 – which perhaps explains the rumour connecting the sacking to an affair.

When I call Kate I'm too chicken to ask at the outset about an affair, but there are plenty of other things to talk about and we get there eventually. Kate's in her early 70s – about a decade younger than Dad would be now. She's clever and chatty, with a spiky, wicked wit. She remembers Dad, and Mum, and the rest of the family, with great fondness. She's full of opinions worth hearing. We're on the phone for an hour and a half.

They met almost as soon as the Duddings got to Christchurch in 1967. Brasch rounded up the literary set for a lunch to welcome the new *Landfall* editor, and Kate was there with her husband, a Caxton employee.

Kate noticed Robin. He wasn't handsome, and he had slightly unfortunate hair that didn't lie properly, and he didn't make a show of himself, but he was somehow still good-

* Actually it isn't, but it'll do for our purposes.

looking and had a quiet confidence of the sort you might overlook. They were in the same car on the way to lunch, Kate in front, Robin in the back, and it was most peculiar how she could feel his *presence*.

They hit it off. After lunch they were somehow the only ones left, stranded without transport, and Kate remembers the pair of them running drunkenly across paddocks to get to another bar where they figured they'd find someone who could give them a lift home.

She had young children and a marriage on the brink of disintegration. She came out to Barnes Road often, sometimes with the kids, but also alone. She got involved in the production of *Landfall* and would stay late into the evening in Dad's study, where the pair of them would talk about books and words, and proofread the next edition together, while Lois popped in occasionally with cups of coffee and pieces of toast to keep them going. Lois was sturdy and calm and carried on, and who knows what she thought about the two of them secluded in there for hours on end. Kate was an occasional artist, too; she designed one of the *Landfall* covers – a hippyish, swirling pattern of buds and petal with a slightly sexual, Georgia O'Keeffe-ish look.

Kate felt Robin was one of the first people – the first man, certainly – to take her seriously. So many men she knew, people like her father, Dinny, couldn't imagine how you could be *friends* with a woman. Women were for the kitchen or the bed and nowhere in between, but Robin saw Kate fully.

'I think Robin sought and needed a female acolyte, a sounding board. We loved some of the same things about books and words. I can remember Robin saying some words and mouthing them, like they were dainty titbits you could eat. He loved the sound of words running together and how they fitted. The poems would come in, and you could tell by the way Robin read them out whether he approved of how the words were strung together or not.'

Family friends. A special bond between Robin and the mother of the other family. Intense conversations about poetry and words. Stoic Lois hanging about the sidelines and not making a fuss. It's as if every couple of years Dad, Mum and an ever-changing Other Woman would pick up the same three-hander script for a read-through.

The obvious question then, again: Was there an affair?

'Well . . .' says Kate, and then gives so many different answers to the question it takes me a while to decide what they add up to.

'We certainly had an emotional and mental affair, if you like, but if you remember, both Adam and Anna were born during the same period, so I wasn't the beneficiary. Besides, I was a dim sort of girl and was frightened to some extent of what my husband would do.

'I loved Robin, but I don't think we had an *affair*. I don't think you could say that, though we were both very fond of each other. But a love affair? Nooooo.

'Perhaps,' she says, laughing, 'we gave it a try but it never worked.'

There were occasions when she and Robin went out together, and one of the horrid things about that era, she says, was that 'people thought if a man and a woman are getting on well and being friendly they must be having sex'.

I get that. But the person who'd told me there was an affair wasn't a 1960s Cantabrian prude; it was my mother – broadminded, non-judgemental Lois – and she'd told me only because I asked. These two versions don't tally.

'Lois must have been fully aware that we were fond of each other,' says Kate. 'But that fondness had far more strings, if you like, than sex. And when you say somebody's had an affair it means they're having sexual thrashings about, and it wasn't like that at all.

'I was very fond of Robin – to me he was the father figure I hadn't had, an older-brother figure I'd never had, an appreciative man I'd never known. He was all of those things to me – of course I was fond of him. Of course I loved him. But not in that way.'

Kate says the relationship, whatever it was, eventually cooled off. She divorced, remarried, and moved to the other side of Christchurch, after which the two families saw less of each other. Lois and Robin produced children numbers five and six. Life went on.

The falling-out at Caxton that saw her father fire Robin was even later still, and she really doesn't think an affair, real or perceived, was a factor. Certainly, none of the many letters written during the Dudding–Donovan stoush contains even a whisper about any impropriety (though arguably it's not the sort of thing anyone would have put in writing).

Kate tells me a bit more about her memories of Dad, about Dinny and the Caxton Press, about the horrors of narrow-minded 1960s Christchurch, and about how she learnt of Dad's death only by reading about it in the *Listener*. I tell her it was emphysema and she agrees he smoked like a trooper. She inquires after all my sisters and asks me to pass on a hug to Mum – 'I would have hated to have hurt Lois'. She says she can hear a bit of Dad's voice in mine, and she recommends Martin Amis's *Experience* if I want to read a good memoir about a father. She says there's a spare room at her house if my family's ever in town. We hang up. I can see why Dad found her good company.

A few days later I tell Mum that Kate sends her regards, and that she's told me there wasn't an affair as such. Mum shrugs and smiles.

'That's not what Robin told me.'

Dad never lost his enthusiasm for literate, attractive young female acolytes, but as he got older and the women he took an interest in stayed much the same age, I suspect their mutual perceptions of what was going on started to part company.

In the 1980s, a time when Dad was frequently ill-tempered with his immediate family, the poet Beth Nannestad was one of the handful of literary visitors still coming to Sealy Road. There were beach walks with Robin, intense conversations about literature, a smiling Lois bringing the coffee and toast – all the usual stuff.

I really liked Beth, but I'd observe with a gimlet eye Dad's courtly attentiveness and bitch about it later with my sisters: how come he's such a miserable, vile-tempered jerk to everyone else but sweetness and light with her? Does she mind his blinking doe-eyes? Why doesn't she find it gross like we do?

I ask Beth if she was aware of how taken Dad was with her back then, and she seems totally startled by the idea. He was just really interested in what I was doing with my poetry, she says.

Carol and Mick Delaney and their kids returned from the UK in 1981 and once again lived around the corner from us. For the most part we picked up where they'd left off, with days at Long Bay and dinner at each other's houses. The Delaneys had a big TV and we still had none, so we'd make family pilgrimages on Sunday evenings to watch the *Brideshead Revisited* mini-series with them.

Carol and Robin were still friendly, even if there wasn't the intense connection of seven years earlier. Then one night, says Carol – she thinks it was probably a New Year's Eve party, when everyone had had a bit to drink – Dad suddenly turned on her. He had an ugly look on his face. He seemed angry. He spat out his words, and said something like: 'What are you doing? You don't know the effect you have on people.'

Carol didn't have a clue what he meant, but she recognised the tone. It was the same snarl she'd heard from Mick when he was in one of his depressive troughs. She thought: Stuff this, I've already got one of those, thank you, and she backed off.

From that day, the lines were redrawn. If Carol rang Sealy Road and Dad answered, he'd grunt 'I'll get Lois' and put the receiver down. If Dad rang the Delaneys and Carol answered, he'd say in a monotone 'Is Mick there?' and wait, saying nothing more.

She and Robin were never friends again. It was quite a feat, considering Robin and Mick remained close mates for decades after that. They jogged and cycled and played badminton, went to films and the pub, talked about books and music and art.

Thirty-five years on, Carol, Mick and Mum say they still don't know exactly what triggered Dad to cut Carol off. But for Carol, it's all there in that Lawrence poem – the one they'd talked about on the sands of Long Bay. Robin had become 'sun-extinct', and was now 'busy putting out the sun / in other people'.

15. The boy with the long hair

Good husbands make unhappy wives
so do bad husbands, just as often;
but the unhappiness of a wife with a good husband
is much more devastating
than the unhappiness of a wife with a bad husband.
– D.H. Lawrence, 'Pansies', 1929

When my sister Anna was 14 and I was 11, she developed a game with her two best friends, Belinda and Natasja, where they would make up outrageous lies about each other and then compete to convince the rest of their class of its truth.

The hands-down winner was Belinda (or perhaps it was Natasja) with her widely accepted claim that the Dudding family were followers of a creepy religious sect which barred them from cutting their hair or their lawns, and in which all the girls were obliged to marry as soon as they turned 16.

As lies go it was hardly a stretch. Anna's classmates had seen her getting dropped at school by her strangely dressed father with his rusty old van and his huge beard, and the notion of an alternative community in the middle of the burbs wasn't that strange. Centrepoint, a bona fide tree-hugging free-love commune, was thriving in nearby Albany (and this was before it became clear that Centrepoint was harbouring a nest of predatory paedophiles who were giving drugs to and having sex with young children). If you walked past the Dudding house at 4 Sealy Road with its rusting Ford Transit parked out front, you could see glimpses, through a vast bamboo hedge, of a front yard utterly lost to shoulder-high weeds and grass. And, sure enough, the countless Dudding children all had really long hair, even the youngest one. The boy who looked like a girl. Me.

I never made a conscious decision to grow my hair long. I'm told that when I was about two Mum asked if I wanted a haircut and I said no, and that was that. Ours was not a compulsory crew cut kind of family, and perhaps I was taking my long-haired sisters as role models. Every few years Mum would politely check if I wanted to cut it yet and I'd always say no, though in her wisdom Mum did hack a wide, crooked fringe for me to see through, which made the style even more emphatically girlish. On my first day at Glamorgan Primary my future best friend Philip clocked the white-blond hair down my back and politely explained that this was actually the boys' toilet – the girls' was across the corridor.

I didn't especially like having long hair. It ended up in my mouth when eating; it blew in my face when riding a bike or walking in the wind; I grew bored of being asked 'Are you a girl or a boy?'; and I didn't much like it when a few months after I started school a large Standard One boy ambushed me on my way home and ordered me to drop my pants to clear up his confusion. It was a drag having to fend off minor and not-so-minor bullying for the first few weeks whenever I started a new school. It also really didn't help that the one sport I turned out to be quite good at was a girly one – gymnastics, where I had to tie my hair in a ponytail to avoid strangling myself on the parallel bars.

Yet by some kind of follicular Stockholm Syndrome the more grief I encountered because of my hair the more determined I became not to lose this mark of distinction. If I capitulated and became a boring, conventional short-hair, all my suffering to that point would have been in vain (something I've since learnt logicians call the sunk-cost fallacy).

I suspect there was one other reason I stuck with my long hair so long, but it was something I couldn't have articulated if I hadn't been interviewing my sisters for this book.

We all knew our family was a bit unusual, and that no one else had an outdoor toilet or a parents' double bed in the living room. We knew other people didn't have holes in their floors and ceilings, or a shower that worked only if you bunged up the bath tap with a whittled-down wine-bottle cork then retightened the loop of baling twine that kept the shower pipe firmly attached to the taps, because if you didn't you were liable to be scalded by horizontal jets of hot water shooting out at knee-level.

Yet although we felt duly embarrassed by those things, by some quirk of confidence we also knew these things made us superior. From our tumbledown shack behind a mad bamboo hedge we sat in judgement of the rest of the world and found it slightly wanting. Looking back, I suspect this misplaced confidence, this feeling that other people were not quite up to snuff, was something we'd learnt from Dad.

He had a knack for reading people, no question. In the same way that he could spot a typo in a sentence or a false note in a poem, he had a knack for noticing people's weak spots – their hypocrisies, their intellectual failings, their physical imperfections. He'd quietly clock them and then, if you were on his team, he might, with the smallest of comments or eyebrow lifts, let you see what he'd just spotted.

Then you'd see it too and without wanting to you'd find yourself thinking a little less of the friend who'd come over after school, or the parents who'd picked them up later. Perhaps that person really was a bit boring, or thoughtless, or bourgeois, or had a sway back, or sandy eyebrows, or was either pregnant or eating too much.

Everyone bitches, but the curious thing about Dad's sledging was that it always seemed so *reasonable*. He wasn't being *critical*; he just couldn't help noticing, ha ha, that this woman was always asking nosey questions, that guy seemed a bit racist, this girl had a face like the back of a bus.

Yeah, you'd think. I hadn't thought of that before, but yeah, that's a good point actually.

He had a way, Melissa says to me, of 'putting people down in a joking way that you knew wasn't really joking'.

'I didn't bring home the first few boyfriends I was interested in,' says Ruth, 'because I knew Dad would see their flaws, and that anything he said would influence me strongly.'

Anna puts it this way: 'I used to think that ours was the only normal family on the planet, because he talked about every other family as being odd, or weird, or off. He'd criticise school friends who were going off to be doctors. He'd imply we were superior to other families for having just the one car and having no money.'

It was only in her teens that Anna started to notice the incongruity: 'I thought, hey, how come everyone is weird but we're not? How come our lawn is so long people think we are a commune – how come that's not weird, yet other people are?'

Having gleaming blond hair down to my bum definitely made me weird, but maybe part of the reason I could shrug off the suggestions from friends and well-meaning adults that my life would be easier if I chopped it off was that I'd decided that being unusual wasn't only OK, it was further proof that I, like my family, was a little bit better than everyone else.

Most summers we visited Dad's parents, Winifred and Ernest, in Hastings, though the only bit I really looked forward to was the inevitable trip to Fantasyland, a theme park with a miniature train and a giant Old Woman's Shoe which you could climb inside, with its own window and thatched roof.

My grandparents' house was chaotic in a similar way to ours – piles of papers and clothes and stuff all over the place – but where our mess was inviting and cosy, to me theirs felt colder, alien.

Grandma was a hoarder. You'd open the fridge to find nine blocks of butter with expiry dates from years before. She'd preserved enough fruit to outlast a nuclear winter, and most meals included a moreish, salty serving of the runner beans that she'd fed through a hand-cranked slicer and preserved in enormous jars of brine at some point in the past half-century. Dad said it was partly a hangover from Depression-era parenting. She was thin and nervy, birdlike, with the same piercing eyes as Dad. She probably cuddled us children, but I don't remember it.

Grandad was usually out in the garden or down in the fowl-run. If inside, he'd be having a nap you weren't allowed to disturb, or he'd be wandering about, recently arisen, in greying singlet and baggy Y-fronts, dispensing nose-flicks, finger-locks and dry-shaves.

My memories of those 1970s visits are a haze of heat and boredom, of blinding sun outside and cool gloom inside, of playing cards and reading till your head felt like cotton-wool, and the stinking hot day when I used my big toes to dig holes in the ponds of half-molten tar that had appeared in the road and Mum perched me on the side of the cement tub in Grandma's outdoor wash-house and tried to scrape off the tar under the hot water.

This was the home where, according to my uncle Ian, my grandmother had sheltered her children against the outside world, taught them to distrust strangers, blocked their contact with all but the small, trusted circle of her immediate relatives.

I can't help wondering if despite his best efforts Dad sometimes got caught in the echoes of Winifred's domestic xenophobia. He'd shrugged off his upbringing to become the warm, generous guy who set up a Friday evening literary salon in his own house, who organised picnics for his entire street, whose door was always open. But some part of him couldn't help feeling, when strangers came to the door, that there was something slightly wrong with most of them.

On the morning of Tuesday 13 November 1980 Dad handed me a small package. Like all birthday and Christmas presents from him it was wrapped in the utilitarian brown paper, shiny one side, matte the other, in which he wrapped bundles of *Islands* for shipment to booksellers. Inside, typed on a slip of tightly folded paper, was a riddle, the first clue in a treasure hunt that led me into the kitchen cutlery drawer, under the piano lid, down to the outside toilet, back inside to the fridge, out to the letterbox and down the sloping garden to the fowl-houses, where one last clue was hiding among the eggs in a straw-filled laying box.

The answer was 'bed'. I carried the slip of paper (and the eggs) back up to the house and there, balanced on its stand on my top bunk with its handlebars scraping the ceiling, was the treasure – a brand new Raleigh 20 for my 10th birthday.

I didn't have the heart to tell Dad that a Raleigh 20, with its skirt-friendly low crossbar and upright handlebars, was dangerously close to being a girl's bike, especially when, like this one, it had a baby-blue frame and white tyres. Still, it was in vastly superior condition to the rusting, broken-chained hand-me-downs that came before it, and when you flicked the pedals backwards it would switch flawlessly between its two gears. I was pretty happy with it.

Over the summer break Mum took me shopping for the uniform for my new school – grey shorts, grey shirts, grey jumper, Roman sandals for the summer months, clompy leather shoes for winter. The sandals came in blue or brown and after some agonising we chose blue, an error whose terrible magnitude became apparent only on my first day at Northcross Intermediate, when I learnt the unwritten code stating brown sandals could be worn by anyone, but blue sandals were strictly for girls. At lunchtime I watched as a small lynch mob gathered to encircle and jeer at a weeping boy who was wearing blue sandals like a total sissy. I stood on the edge of the crowd, guiltily aware that someone ought to stick up for this loser, but also anxious that no one discover the pair of blue sandals just like his in my schoolbag, where they'd been safely hidden since before the 9 o'clock bell. I had girl's hair. I had a girl's bike. I'd spent the day telling a new cohort of classmates that the reason I was wearing a boy's uniform was that I was indeed a boy. I was buggered if I was going to get caught wearing girl's sandals as well.

A few weeks into my first term at Northcross, Dad suddenly announced we were all going to Hastings to see his father. A smoker who'd also spent a lifetime inhaling flour at the bakery, Ernest had begun to suffer from asthma in his 70s. Dad told us he'd just had a particularly bad attack and was in hospital. It looked like it might be serious.

The two oldest Dudding girls were no longer living at home, but by the Saturday afternoon the rest of us were in the blue Transit, heading south on State Highway 1. We broke the journey with an overnight stay with friends in Taupo – a big mistake, as it turned out. When we pulled up outside Grandad's place on Sunday morning Dad's brother-in-law Ray, Ngaire's husband, was waiting for us at the gate.

'You're too late,' he said. Grandad had had another asthma attack in hospital. He had died five hours earlier. Out in the back garden Ngaire was already burning Grandad's old clothes in the 40-gallon-drum incinerator.

Dad had always disliked his brother-in-law Ray, but from that day he loathed him – for appointing himself the messenger even though he wasn't immediate family, for waiting at the gate and telling us before we'd even got out of the van, for being so puffed up with self-importance as he swaggered over to give us the news. Ray himself died a few months later of a heart attack.

We got back into the Transit and drove to the hospital. Ernest lay grey on a gurney, a sheet covering him from chest down. Dad put his hand on his dead father's shoulder and spoke. I remember he said something about getting there too late, but not much else. Perhaps he said something about the ridiculous fight they'd had about a stupid mail-order coat the last time they saw each other.

It was the first dead body I'd seen, and the first time I'd seen Dad cry.

Whenever my sisters and I talked about what went wrong for Dad in the 1980s, we usually agreed that the day Grandad died was a turning point – day one of the descent – even if we couldn't quite understand why it had had such a profound effect. (After Dad himself died, I warily waited for a couple of years to see if history would repeat. Maybe every son is meant to go a little mad after the death of his father.)

Now, with the benefit of a hard-drive full of letters and a recorder full of interviews, I'm still certain something snapped the day Ernest died. But now I see it wasn't so much a sudden change as a final straw. After decades of surviving on anxiety and cigarettes, of turning a blind eye to financial realities, of setting himself impossible deadlines and missing them, of castigating himself for working when he should have been with his family and for being with his family when he should have been working, of fretting about unmown lawns and the leaking roof, Dad was at last derailed by the death of his father.

Professionally, the 1970s had been a great decade. He'd placed himself at the centre of the country's literature with *Landfall* then *Islands* and published some award-winning books on the side (including Kevin Ireland's *Literary Cartoons*). He'd earned the respect of the kind of people whose opinion he respected. He'd won a brief fellowship at Auckland University and been gifted a lovely big IBM electric typewriter as part of a Literary Fund grant.

And despite the holes in shoes and roof, he'd been incredibly lucky with money, from Charles Brasch's deep backing of *Islands*, to the profitable sale of the Christchurch house that meant the house in Torbay was all but mortgage-free.

The real financial miracle, though, had been in 1974, when Dad won $15,000 from the Bonus Bonds account where he banked *Islands* subscribers' cheques. This was a vast sum, the equivalent of three or four years of a mid-range salary, and it sustained for several more years Dad's impossible dream: that he could produce *Islands* more or less fulltime and still keep us fed. There was even enough money to build an extension to the house in 1978 – a sun-deck, an extra bedroom and an indoor study for himself – though naturally the budget was wildly optimistic and the money ran out, leaving gib-board walls unplastered and unpainted, doors and windows without handles or latches and the floors unvarnished, which is how they all remained for the next 25 years.

By the turn of the decade, though, the Bonus Bonds win was long gone and he was faced with an unavoidable reality: a literary magazine, no matter how well-loved and supported by Arts Council grants and the occasional philanthropic cheque, will seldom cover its own costs, let alone generate enough money to feed the editor and his family, especially an editor as slow and painstaking as Robin Dudding. And Dudding kept getting slower and slower and slower.

Three months after the death of his father, Dad published *Islands* 31/32, a desperate double issue designed to make up for years of slippage between intended and actual publication dates.* And then the machine stopped, and *Islands* died – or rather, slipped into a deep coma, where it would remain for three years.

Dad was thousands of dollars in debt to printers, and was struggling to pay household bills. He had plenty of material for future editions but could afford neither to produce them nor to call it quits and return everybody's subscription and his Arts Council grants. He found himself, as he wrote to a friend, 'unable to earn enough to keep us, even at our smell-of-an-oily-rag level – which I'm heartily sick of'. He had, he

---

* Unlike the unashamedly occasional *Mate*, *Islands* followed the rigid nomenclature of a proper quarterly: four issues a year – Autumn, Winter, Spring and Summer – comprising a single 'volume' with continuous page numbering across the issues. This makes it easy to track the difference between the intended season of publication printed on each *Islands* spine ('Autumn 1974' etc) and the actual month of publication on the title page. I put both sets of dates into a spreadsheet, with a third column recording the difference – a pitilessly empirical measure of the distance between intention and reality.

In 1974 the lag is nil. Two years later *Islands* 15 has 'Autumn 1976' on the spine and 'September 1976' inside – four months late by the most generous interpretation of seasons. The lag hits eight months in 1977 before edging back to five months in late 1978. In 1979, in a desperate move that must have fooled nobody, Dad redefines the five editions of 1978 and 1979 as a single, two-year volume (an oxymoron, really) and drops the telltale seasons from the spine. With the calendar reset the first two editions of 1980 are on time, but the third is a month late, and there's no fourth edition at all that year.

In 1981 another calendrical sleight of hand – a double issue that claims simultaneously to complete the previous year's volume and kick off the current year's. It's disastrously late, even with the benefit of dubious labelling. Depending on how charitably you do the maths, when *Islands* 31/32 is published in June 1981 it's somewhere between three and 15 months late.

wrote, 'ballsed things up pretty badly [. . .] the range goes from the domestic to the literary I might say'.

I was 10, and mostly oblivious to the professional and financial disasters around me. For years Mum and Dad had made an oily rag seem a perfectly reasonable basis for a household economy. I thought everyone bought petrol in $5 sips rather than filling the tank. I really didn't care that my school uniform and satchel were hand-me-downs from my piano teacher's son, or that Mrs Hungerford gave deeply discounted rates for Anna and my lessons. I remember once looking at the Golden Kiwi lottery ticket magneted to our fridge and asking Dad why he bothered buying them. We didn't need more money than we had, did we?

And though Dad may have been in a state of panic as he sat at his typewriter, with me he seemed much the same as ever. We ran up and down Long Bay Beach, training for the Round the Bays fun run along Tamaki Drive according to the daily schedule printed in the *Auckland Star*. We also paid close attention to the *Star*'s pseudo-scientific biorhythm charts, noting the days that we were meant to be in optimal Physical, Emotional or Intellectual condition. We wrestled on the couch. I was still small enough for the occasional piggyback. We played balloon soccer up and down the sitting room, occasionally breaking light fittings.

At intermediate I was learning that having long hair wasn't all bad. The deputy principal, a clever but thuggish man called Penn McKay, called me Adam Fawcett-Majors, which I chose to take as a compliment. A few months into the year everyone in the school who'd wondered if I was a girl or a boy had already asked me, and the art teacher Mrs Storm said if I ever cut my hair off she'd happily buy it to use on the

Victorian-style dolls she made as a sideline.

I could tell that I was nearing the point when I would no longer let Dad hold my hand when we crossed a road, but I still let him occasionally. I liked being with him. He was still nice to me. What was bothering me, though, was the way he'd started being strangely unpleasant towards my mother.

16. Moving the furniture back

Mum served dinner and called Anna, Dad and me to the table. I don't remember what it was, but perhaps it was brown rice with a bit of onion and garlic and some rubbery strips of pan-fried steak, or maybe it was watery mashed potatoes with watery boiled mince and watery overcooked cabbage.

It wasn't that Mum was a bad cook. When we had weekend visitors she'd get an apron on and cover the table with a spread of salads from the garden, homemade bread, boiled eggs, sliced cheese, fried rice, vegetable soup, bowls of peanuts and sultanas. But on weeknights her heart wasn't in it, and who could blame her? The squeezed grocery budget meant there was never anything fancy in the fridge, the stove usually had several broken elements and her own healthy-eating puritanism meant cans, packets and frozen foods were out of the question – as were, for the most part, salt, butter, sugar, white flour, MSG-laden stock cubes and other wicked shortcuts to palatability.

More importantly, though, Mum would rather be reading a book or sitting in the garden than stuck in our tiny, squalid kitchen, so she'd wander off mid-preparation then scramble to put things right when she remembered she was making a meal. Some dishes suited this approach – an Irish stew, tasty and swimming with bits of spud and carrot and chunks of falling-apart chuck steak, say, or baked potatoes with a casseroled piece of meat.

The nightmare possibility, though, was if she decided to do anything involving lentils or kidney beans, which would end up in a steaming faecal pile on your plate, desperately under-flavoured except for a strong cindery taint. Without fail she would have put them on to boil and remembered them only when smoke was curling under the door into the sitting room. The incinerated bottom layer would be scraped into the compost bin but the smoky remainder would be salvaged and served.

Whatever it might have been that evening, we ate it. Then Anna or I cleared the table and Mum reappeared with the next course, which might have been apple crumble, or stewed peaches with a sponge topping, or bread-and-butter pudding, or maybe just a bowl of stewed apple.

'Here you go,' she said cheerily, handing round the served plates. 'Dessert!'

Dad glanced at the bowl then back up at Mum. His face twisted. He scraped his chair back and stood, cheeks suddenly bright red, eyes narrowed.

'It's not fucking *dessert*,' he roared. 'It's pudding.'

He took the bowl and smashed it to the floor. Then he vanished through the double-doors leading to the garden and his office.

Mum widened her eyes. She bent down and gathered up the pieces of smashed plate and scattered globs of dessert, pudding, what-fucking-ever, and carried them to the kitchen bin. Anna and I soldiered on with our spoons. The food suddenly didn't taste of much, but we were used to forcing down meals without much appetite.*

Actual plate-smashing was a rare excitement, so extreme and absurd that Anna and I – the last two kids still living at home – could giggle about it as soon as Dad had stalked from the room. Another explosion, when he threw an egg at Mum and it smashed and dripped down her face, became funny a week after the event but was nasty at the time.

Far more common, though, was for Dad to sit through a meal in stony-faced silence, seething in anger over God only knows what, filling the room with a sour, buzzing tension, a possibility of violence. He might say nothing at all, or snarl a brief complaint about the toughness of the lamb chops, or just give an angry sigh. After he'd eaten he'd stand and leave the room.

I suspect the reason mealtimes in particular were so tense was that they were the one time Dad was forced into close proximity to Mum. The rest of the day he could avoid her, timing his movements so they were never in the same room for long. They'd become like a pair of repelling magnets, able to draw close only with the greatest of effort for brief, unstable moments.

---

* Later, Anna and I tried to figure out the etymology of Dad's rage. Given his disdain for airs and graces, we figured he must have considered the word 'dessert' a snobby variant of the more honest, proletarian 'pudding', though my recent googling on the subject suggests if that's the case he had it back to front. In the UK at least, it seems 'dessert' is the below-stairs term, and posh people say 'pudding'.

Sometimes he literally wouldn't talk to her for months on end, apart from brief pretences for the benefit of visitors. If Mum tried to engage him in conversation he'd make a dash for the door.

For someone who loved conversation as much as Mum did, silent treatment was especially cruel. Many years later, my sisters and I would find in Dad's office a letter she'd written him during one of those silences. It's a short note but there's a lot there: anger, despair, frustration, hope, flattery, flirtation.

> I hesitate to write to you as I have a fear of being misunderstood and do not like the thought of you finding signs of arrogance or blind egoism or similar but what the hell – here goes (our lack of 'meeting' couldn't be worse than it is and I feel your opinion of me couldn't be lower.)
>
> If you want to have a really good fight we'll have to make some rules first, because our exchanges do not keep to the point and the irrelevant digs just make things worse.
>
> You have asked me to make a list of points for discussion. I think I have told you what worries me, often enough, but if I haven't made it clear here they are.
>
> Money.
>
> Work & occupation.
>
> The thing that bothers me most – (us) is not exactly a matter for discussion as I think it is a state or summat.
>
> All the other things – the house – travel, chores etc are just daily things to negotiate about – like what to have for dinner.
>
> But this wasn't written to make lists about problems but mainly to say hello and to get you to say hello back. If I were to say that I liked your tender and crisp cabbages your

luxuriant lettuce and the way you get parsley to grow like nobody's business you might think I'm a liar.

You might also say I've got an ulterior motive if I say how pretty the bantams are and how elegant your bamboo. Well, too bad! Most of the nicest things between us I don't like writing down because it immediately becomes just a bit less private. Anyway that's all for now.

It's a love letter really, if a profoundly depressing one, though the sentences about cabbages and lettuce make me laugh: just because she was miserable didn't mean Mum was going to pass up the opportunity for some alliteration.

Dad must have seen the note. He could read a text on its surface and underneath. He wasn't stupid. I'd love to know what went through his head as he read this letter from the woman he lived with. At the time, it looked like he hated her – found her very existence intolerable. I couldn't understand why, and I still don't, exactly.

Certainly she had a handful of irritating qualities. She would tell terminally digressive anecdotes, so exquisitely boring that we'd either beg her to stop or just glaze over, totally forgetting she was even talking ('*. . . so it was on Friday . . . no it can't have been on the Friday because I had just been to the shops . . . and I was talking to Pat . . . so surely it was Thursday . . . no, perhaps it was Friday after all, because . . .*').

She was also near-incapable of giving a direct yes/no answer to such tricky questions as 'Would you like another biscuit?' ('*Well . . . I've already had one. That's probably enough. Ooh they are good though. Would you like one? Shall I put the kettle on? . . .*').

She was always, *always* late leaving the house, so Dad

would just leave when he was ready and sit in the car, listening to the radio as she faffed around looking for her shoes or her other glasses for another half an hour or more.

Yet, as Anna and I reasoned as we tried to solve the Mystery of the Increasingly Unpleasant Father, none of these was a capital crime. Also, she'd been like that ever since we could remember and Dad had only started getting nasty recently, so whether she was annoying or not wasn't really the point. However we looked at it, Dad was the villain.

Their marriage had never been equal as such, but there'd been a tacit contract that had functioned for years. Robin brought home the bacon and Lois cooked it. Robin brought fascinating, creative people into the Duddings' orbit and Lois made them lunch and cups of coffee and took part in the clever conversations. Robin dreamt up fun things to do – camping holidays in Coromandel, a summer barbecue at Long Bay for the entire street – and Lois made the logistics work, minded the kids, cooked the food, had a good time.

Robin made the decisions, drove the only vehicle, controlled the money. Lois went with the flow, let the driving licence she'd got in her teens lapse and seemed to accept that the only money she'd ever handle was the cash Dad gave her each week for groceries.

If there was a bit of spare money, Robin might pick out a nice dress from a shop, and Lois would wear it. It never occurred to him that she might want to pick one herself. He liked her hair long, and when she cut it short once he flew into a small rage before apologising with a bunch of flowers. He didn't like her wearing make-up, though she'd still venture a dab of lipstick for fancy occasions.

During our cheese-quiche lunch, Carol Delaney reminds

Mum of the time she'd done Mum's make-up for her – the full mid-1970s nine yards with plenty of eye shadow and mascara. When Dad saw the transformation he was furious and scolded Carol.

'What's wrong?' asked Carol. 'She wanted to pretty herself up.'

'She doesn't need prettying up,' said Dad.

If Carol's husband had tried to control her like that she'd have told him where he could shove the lipstick, but Mum wasn't like that. She knew she'd ceded too much territory to Robin somewhere along the line, but didn't quite know how to claim it back.

She sometimes told a story about the time, before they'd had their first child, when Dad had headed off to the *Auckland Star* and she'd decided to make something of the day and rearrange the furniture in their one-room Herne Bay flat. When Dad got home he wasn't angry exactly, but he told her she'd made a mistake and the couch and the armchair and the little table must be returned to where they were when he left for work.

That was the moment, Mum would say 30 or so years after the event, when she should have told him to get stuffed. That's when she should have pointed out that in a real partnership both people get to make decisions about the optimal angling of chairs. At the very least she should have calmly said: 'Move them yourself, darling.' But she didn't. Instead she smiled bravely and put everything back like he said.

And now the deal, with its balance between control and kindness, was breaking down. The housekeeping budget had become impossibly small as Dad's professional life grew more chaotic. The stream of literary visitors had become a trickle and if Mum had the temerity to invite friends she'd made for herself Dad would greet them with the same mix of hostile silence or muttered insults he was perfecting on her. And he was losing his knack for creating fun: a summer camping trip when I was 12 was the last family holiday we took.

There were better days and worse days, better years and worse years. But if I zoom out enough to see the whole of the 1980s at a glance, it's all of a piece. This was the decade that Dad stopped being nice.

Traits that had been mildly irritating, or even entertainingly quirky, took on a darker tone. That early control-freakery about the placement of furniture metastasised into a generalised anger at anyone's attempts to move or change anything at all in his house. Every pile of two-month-old newspapers, every little mound of shorts and underpants discarded on the dining table en route to his evening bath, every pair of chook-shit-spattered gumboots left just inside the front door, attracting flies – dare to tidy them away and he'd walk about bellowing: 'Who moved my newspapers/pants/boots?!' For a couple of decades an entire wall of the living room was ramparted by stacks of cardboard boxes containing thousands of misprinted or unsold back issues of *Islands*, vaguely camouflaged with draped bed-sheets. They weren't to be touched, moved, or talked about.

He exerted the same grip over his outdoor domain: if Mum dared plant a few daffodil bulbs alongside a garden path there was every chance Dad would dig them back up the same day. Didn't she realise that was where he'd been planning to put some dahlias? And why had she moved his gardening fork anyway?

For several years there was a metre-wide hole in the kitchen floor where the leaking sink had rotted the boards. Dad's solution was to take a cupboard door that had fallen off its hinges and balance it over the hole. He never did dishes so was in little personal danger, but Mum did, and one day the door wobbled and flipped as she stood on it, and she fell through to the dirt a metre below, hurting her leg. The door was retrieved and rebalanced and the hole remained.

Eventually Melissa's boyfriend Brett turned up with a large sheet of chipboard, some nails and a belt of tools and spent a day building a new section of floor. Dad's reaction was exactly what we all expected – insult and outrage. Hadn't he said that he was just about to fix it himself? Couldn't we see that Brett had made a terrible hash of it? Look – the new piece of wood didn't sit flush with the old boards, and the unsealed chipboard was only going to swell up when it got splashed.

It was the same reaction he gave to all the acts of guerrilla DIY committed by his children or their partners in the 80s and 90s in the hope of making Sealy Road slightly more habitable. Ruth swooped in to replace a crumbling kitchen sink-top that came away in little chips of stone if you tried to wipe it clean. Natasha's teenage boyfriend noticed the scrolls of peeling paint, black with mould, that curled like parchment from the living-room ceiling and insisted on stripping and painting it; he was never forgiven by Dad.

Ten years on, the ceiling was black and peeling once more so a high school friend and I repeated the exercise. Dad moaned for weeks: what was the point of painting the ceiling while there was still a leak in the roof that he had been just about to fix? Why had we bought new brushes when there were some perfectly serviceable ones in the shed that just needed a bit of soaking? Why hadn't I asked his permission before painting His Ceiling? (He was very clear about the ownership of Sealy Road. Mum once referred to 'our house' mid-argument, and he corrected her. 'It's not *our* house,' he said of the place where she and he raised six children together over a quarter of a century. 'It's *my* house.')

He wasn't incapable of DIY. He could replace a pane of glass and build a set of bookshelves or a chicken coop. He could whittle a champagne cork to the right shape to make a bung for the bath tap's shower attachment. When we went on a long camping holiday and he nailed the front door shut so the house was safe from burglars, seeing it didn't have a lock, he didn't hit his thumb with the hammer. It's just that every task had to join a queue and be done in the right order, *his* order, and he was busy right now and Somebody Had Moved His Tools Again.

He became slightly grumpy most of the time with most people, but, when his free-floating ill-temper focussed enough to find a specific target, it was usually Mum.

I was frequently outraged on her behalf, and because she was an exceptionally tolerant listener, she'd let me rant on about Dad's failings with all the indignation a know-it-all teenager can summon: he was an arsehole; he showed no sign of becoming nice again; his most recent tantrum was the last straw; she needed to escape this oppression; she must leave him. She'd never endorse my hectoring out loud, but I could tell she didn't entirely disagree.

Yet she didn't leave. Instead, she read self-help books. *Women Who Love Too Much. You Can Heal Your Life. The*

Inner Game of Tennis. I skimmed the books out of curiosity and some of them seemed sensible enough, but *You Can Heal Your Life* was particularly offensive – bestselling New Age bullshit which claimed that AIDS, cancer and being born into poverty were actually all your fault. So sometimes, if I was on a roll, Mum would get two adolescent rants rolled into one: *Leave Dad!* and *Stop Reading Louise L. Hay!*

It never occurred to me that it could work the other way round – that perhaps it was Dad who should leave Mum. Sealy Road, with its disregard for fashion and its pathological levels of disorder, was as much an expression of the inner world of Robin Dudding as those magazines he created.

Dodgy plumbing and holes in the floor; sketches by famous artists Sellotaped to the wall; more books than anyone could ever read; chickens and dogs and cats; plum and peach, tamarillo and guava and loquat, bamboo and cabbage tree and rimu and kōwhai and kauri, planted by him; a dark ravine in the crook of the section where water from a small stream trickling through suburban backyards had eaten away at the earth beneath for years until one winter it collapsed – Sealy Road *was* Robin Dudding.

Yet he did consider fleeing. My sister Ruth told me that in the early 80s when she was at drama school in Wellington, Dad would ring and write letters, and he said enough that she knew things weren't good at home, and one time he really shocked her.

'He said to me – and I think he was almost wanting us to take sides somehow – but he said, "I'm thinking of moving to the Hawke's Bay with Adam, to be with my mother."

'He wanted to take you away from Mum and live with you

somewhere else. I just thought, how on earth could you think about taking Adam away from Mum?'

Thirty years on, it's the first I've heard of such a plan. I'm astonished, but guiltily pleased that he'd have wanted to take me with him. Not that I'd ever have wanted to go. Exchange Auckland and Mum and my entire life to date for Hastings and my strange, sharp-edged grandmother? No thanks.

The toxic atmosphere at home was just another reason, on top of the outdoor loo and the double bed in the living room, not to bring friends home. But when I wasn't physically in the same room as the two combatants, I mainly forgot about it. I had other things to worry about: armpit hair, masturbation, acne, friends, bullies, unrequited crushes, school productions, band practices.

It helped that other kids at school seemed to have parents whose relationships were just as bad. There were separations and divorces. One day a friend told me that over the weekend he'd pointed a loaded .22 rifle at his dad – a respectable businessman with a big car and a big boat and a secretary he'd eventually leave his wife for – to stop him beating up his mum. There were other stories: about the two teachers who'd left their partners to publicly legitimise the affair their pupils had been speculating about for years; the music teacher who'd recently taken a lesbian lover while her husband had moved into a shed in the garden; the kid whose father had killed himself over the summer break. By comparison I didn't feel at all sorry for myself.

Slightly more vexing than tensions at home were the day-to-day hazards of being a teenage boy with long hair at a new school, and a bit of a swot. It didn't take long to spot who represented the greatest threat – a dozen or so free-wheeling kids from the semi-rural town of Paremoremo, some of whose parents were prison guards at the maximum security prison there.

Each Monday, news would filter through the form of how they'd spent their weekend: breaking windows or stealing and crashing their parents' cars perhaps, or chasing the younger brother of one of them – a backward boy called Ozzy – through the bush while hitting him with sticks. One Monday morning they were especially excited because they'd taken the game to the next level by tying a rope around him and hanging him from a tree (by his neck, they said, but given that Ozzy was still alive, I took that part with a grain of salt).

I kind of liked them – they were funny and reckless, and there was an inspired creativity to their pursuit of violence. They invented a variation on the old tennis-ball 'branding' game. The rules were simple: everyone lined up facing a wall and bent over double, then the person with the tennis ball threw it as hard as he could at the row of upraised grey-shorted arses in an act of symbolic buggery/infection (though they didn't put it that way exactly). They called this game 'AIDS', in honour of the newly famous disease.

This was the era of Pac-Man, so at lunchtime the classroom became the maze and they were Pac-Men, and they'd shuffle around in a crab crawl between the rows of desks, kicking the shit out of each other when they intersected. When they tired of that they attached dart flights to their compass needles and hiffed them at each other across the room, a recreation finally banned after a girl walked through the door mid-game and got a needle lodged deep in her thigh.

They were so busy hurting each other that their harassment of me was half-hearted at best. I cut off all my hair the summer I turned 13, not because of bullying but because the next school musical was going to be *South Pacific* and I was in the chorus. I figured I'd still be the second-shortest boy in my year, with an unbroken treble voice, but if I was dancing about the stage dressed as an American GI while singing 'There Is Nothing Like a Dame', it would probably be best if I looked nothing like a dame myself. Also, some of my friends were finding girlfriends and I wasn't. I figured my hair wasn't helping.

Even after the haircut there must have been some bullying, because in Fourth Form I remember leading a small deputation of class goodie-goodies to the form dean, to say we were getting kinda sick of compass-stabs, ankle-taps, screwed-up paper missiles and suchlike. Could he make it stop?

The dean shrugged.

'The thing you need to understand,' he said, 'is that these boys will be gone by Fifth Form. Most won't pass School Certificate. Just wait – in two years they'll all be panel beaters or something and you guys will be left alone.'

We were deeply unimpressed by his lack of pastoral care (and if we'd given a shit about the future of the Paremoremo kids, we'd have been appalled at the school's lack of ambition for them), but with few options left we shrugged at the dean and tolerated another couple of years of low-grade sadistic tomfoolery. By the end of Fifth Form they had, as the dean had predicted, all left school.

When I was 13 Mum started looking for paid work for the first time in 25-odd years. There were some humiliating false starts, like the café that let her go after a week because she was too slow: her idea of carving ham was to meticulously whittle every last molecule of meat from the bone just like she would have at home, when the manager wanted her just to slice the damn thing, fast.

The saga of the paper run was almost as pitiful. In a rare instance of cooperation, Dad and Mum took on a badly paid contract to drop off bundles of the local paper for paperboys and -girls to deliver. The Transit was long broken down and rusting in the front lawn, but Dad had inherited his father's horrible little Ford Thames panel-van. Twice a week they'd fill it with *North Shore Times Advertiser*s, then, as Dad swerved through suburban streets, Mum would sit in the back, reading the address labels and lugging the bundles out the back. Prone to carsickness at the best of times and paranoid about the health effects of petrol fumes, Mum was intensely nauseous within minutes of the first run, and the enterprise was abandoned in less than a fortnight.

Eventually she found her niche, working at the University Bookshop in the city. She knew books and was good at the job. She made a few friends of her own. She even had a little money for a change – though not much, seeing as Dad reduced his own contribution to her weekly housekeeping by the exact amount she was earning.

He joked about it in a letter to family friends ('We struggle on: Lois is breadwinner . . .'), but the shifting power balance clearly bothered him, and when a few years later Mum lifted her sights still further and took a course in teaching English to Speakers of Other Languages (ESOL), he began a startlingly vicious campaign to fuck her up.

By now I was in my first year of university, still living at home because it was cheap and the path of least resistance.

I was the last bird in the nest – even Emma the Labrador-Alsatian had left us, buried in the front lawn under a 'Whisky' rose.

The ESOL syllabus was hardly a stretch for someone as sharp and literate as Mum – the real challenge was finding somewhere to study in peace. Forget a room of one's own; she just wanted a clear surface to put her books. But Dad's doctrine of total ownership made that all but impossible.

Eventually she excavated a couple of square metres in a corner next to the wall of *Islands* boxes and set up a tiny wooden side table as her desk. But once she was out of the house, Dad tipped her stuff – pens, papers, ESOL texts and all – onto the floor. He'd suddenly needed somewhere to put his tomato seedlings, so when Mum got home her former work desk was out in the garden, covered in punnets of sprouting Moneymakers.

As the final practical assessment drew near, Dad stepped up the psychological warfare. Like a rogue state playing deafening martial music across the DMZ, he switched to noisier expressions of hostility – stomping feet, slamming doors, shouting. I don't remember the pretexts for the one-sided fights he'd pick with Mum, but I remember his roaring and his red cheeks and bulging eyes, and the tightness in my chest when I entered the house after a day at uni.

My sister Melissa was doing the same teaching course as Mum and lived nearby, so the night before Mum was required to teach a practicum class under the gaze of an assessor she fled to Melissa's house, hoping for one final evening's prep to make up for the weeks lost to Dad's sabotage.

Some hope. I eavesdropped as Dad rang Melissa and gave her a message to pass on to Lois: 'Tell her if she doesn't fucking come home now she needn't come home at all.'

Mum came home. The next day she failed the assessment. She didn't have enough money to repeat the course.

I was always on Mum's side during our decade of cold war. I had no doubt Dad was at fault. Yet part of me also wondered, with a gut-twist of disloyalty, if the problem was also that she was a bit weak and pathetic; that she should've had the courage to stand up to him, or leave. And maybe she failed that exam not because of Dad, but because she wasn't quite as clever as we'd all assumed. After all, how hopeless do you have to be to get fired from a job making sandwiches in a café?

But endurance is strength too. Despite the humiliations Mum didn't curl up and die. Without a teaching certificate she couldn't get a job at a language school so she took private students at home, a string of tongue-tied Koreans who'd turn up at the front door blinking at the strangeness and clutter of Sealy Road before sidling to a corner of the room to work quietly on their Rs. Dad was unfailingly rude to them and would take strategic strolls through the living room wearing only underpants, but he stopped short of full-scale sabotage.

Mum committed other small acts of defiance. She resuscitated her maiden name in correspondence, and kept doing it even after Dad took the letters from the bank addressed to Lois Miller Dudding and threw them on the floor, saying 'This person doesn't exist.'

After years of sort-of wanting to be vegetarian, she one day announced that henceforth she really was. For a while she kept preparing the chooks Dad had killed but eventually she drew a line and said she would cook them only if someone else got them ready. Dad said gutting and plucking were Mum's jobs, so he stopped killing chooks and we stopped eating chicken altogether.

A few years after the ESOL debacle Mum started taking university papers part time. At the age of 58 she completed the arts degree she'd begun four decades earlier, back when she'd noticed an interesting, nervy young guy with dark hair and an air force uniform up in the front row of her English lectures.

By the time she graduated in 1993 I was overseas, but Ruth and Rachel and Mum's mother went to watch her getting capped and to take her to lunch in the city. Dad had something else he needed to do that day.

When I was younger, my parents would sometimes stand hugging in the middle of the room for long enough that I could clamber aboard, climb up the exterior of the hug and insert myself in its middle. Metaphors for where you want to be in relation to your parents don't get much more straightforward.

By the early 80s there weren't any hugs left to climb into. I was getting too big anyway. Instead I settled for enjoying my parents one at a time.

With Mum it was mainly talk – about what I was learning at school or university, about the merits of Louise L. Hay, about Dad's latest outrage, about her ESOL course, about the world. With Dad it was mainly action – we ran, we swam, we gardened, we read proofs.

Between intermittent issues of *Islands* he took on freelance copy-editing jobs, so we'd spend weekends and evenings in his study making note of where the commas fell in a history of Auckland University, or a book about Captain Cook's interpreter Omai, or James Belich's book about the New Zealand land wars, or a biography of A. R. D. Fairburn (its author Denys Trussell would occasionally visit and play out-of-tune Beethoven sonatas on our piano). One job, copy-editing an exhaustive natural history of dragonflies for Auckland University Press, appalled and fascinated us both with its tender descriptions of the extraordinary variety of ways in which different dragonfly species fuck, often on the wing.

We were on shakier ground if we moved from doing to talking. Dad's treatment of Mum was a wiggly tooth I couldn't leave alone, and most conversations seemed to drift back to my favourite subject: Why are you such a prick to Mum?

He'd never take the bait. He'd neither deny the accusation nor give me the satisfaction of acknowledging he might indeed be at fault. He'd just endure the niggling, waiting till I grew bored with the subject so we could get back to doing stuff.

For reasons I never understood, Anna, the last sister to leave home, couldn't get away with the goading of Dad that I could. If Anna passed comment on Dad's latest mistreatment of Mum he'd snap back at her with the same sudden, intimidating rage he reserved mainly for Mum. Not that it stopped Anna.

One dinnertime, when Anna was 17 and I was 14, she announced she was planning to go on the pill. I suppose she thought that the kind of progressive parents who left copies of *The Joy of Sex* lying around, and who'd already met and liked her first serious boyfriend, would respect such openness and honesty. Mum possibly did, but Dad flinched, and turned to Anna and snarled: 'And where will you *contort* yourselves?' before getting up and leaving the room.

Your teenage years are when you're meant to notice parents aren't the godlike figures you'd once imagined – it's your evolutionary programming telling you it's time to leave the nest – individuate, grow up – isn't it? Somehow, though, at the same time as I was figuring out the precise composition and dimensions of my father's flaws, I grew over-fond of the feeling of righteous indignation that went with it. I found myself almost incapable of talking to him except to criticise him, and over time we settled into twin ruts – querulous complaint on my part, mute wounded dignity on his – and we never quite climbed back out of them.

Except one time. In 1991, not long after I'd left home, and just before I headed abroad for the first time, we met and drank beer at the London Bar in central Auckland, the only time in my life I can recall where both of us were moderately drunk in the same place at the same time.

Dad hardly ever drank and on the handful of times I'd seen him have more than a couple of beers I didn't like the result. There was the time he got hammered on a bottle of rum with a son-in-law and started slurrily swearing at Mum with a nasty glint in his eye. Another time he had quite a few beers and became exaggeratedly tender and sweet towards her, which I found equally disturbing.

When I interviewed Kevin Ireland about the 1950s Queens Ferry days, he talked about how even among the bohemians of the day it was understood that a man mustn't talk about anything too intimate. Dad's inability to talk about personal things was something he shared with most men of his generation, said Kevin, but you were allowed to bend the rules with the help of alcohol.

'When we opened a bottle of beer, Bob was open.'

For some reason it was like that the night I spent with Dad at the London Bar, with the Phil Broadhurst trio crashing its brilliant way through some bebop standard in the corner. I don't remember much of what we said, but I remember that it was fun, and it was easy, and I didn't feel my usual need to harangue him.

I remember he asked me, with an intensity which made me feel the answer really mattered to him – that it was perhaps similar to a question he'd once asked himself – whether I was genuinely excited about trying to make a living playing music, or whether it was just something to do for the time being.

I remember we talked about the fact that I'd recently, finally, belatedly, got round to finding a girlfriend, putting to rest his vague fear that the reason I was taking so long was that I was gay, and we talked about whether having a girlfriend was turning out to be a good thing or not.

Then he said something so far outside our usual conversational lines that it stuck in my mind long after the rest of the night faded.

'I may have fucked up my own,' he said, 'but I do still believe in marriage.'

And that's it – the sum total of what my father ever said to me about the dark cloud that had settled over our family a decade earlier.

Not long after that I went overseas for a few years. Occasionally, much later, I'd try to get him to say more, to tell me about how he'd met Mum, or what it had been like at *Landfall*, or what went so wrong with his life and marriage and career around the time his father died, or why, really, he'd been like that to Mum, but he'd always let the questions slip away.

I knew I should get him back to a bar, to see if opening a few more bottles of beer would open Bob up again, but somehow I kept putting it off, and 17 years passed, and then one day it was too late.

17. Some tentative theories as to the cause of the midlife decline of Robin Dudding

He was depressed, of course, and to ask what *caused* his depression may be pointless, given that the truth probably lies in intractable things like brain chemistry and genetics. That said, here are some speculations on the matter.

Too much gloomy New Zealand literature.
Through the 60s, 70s and 80s, Kevin Ireland tells me, much New Zealand writing was serious and mock-virtuous and gloomy, so joyless and grey you might call it Polish New Zealand Writing. 'I have a feeling that Bob's unrestricted diet of these things produced the reaction that you'd expect, which is every now and then he must have felt a kind of despair.'

Too little money.
Though of course, says Kevin, the underlying problem was always financial. Bob would have made *Islands* forever if he'd had the cash. The Arts Council subsidised the second-rate *Landfall* yet wouldn't give him more for his first-class magazine, and there weren't the big private patrons you get abroad. Bob just needed a dollop of cash and to be left to get on with it.

Too many cigarettes.
And don't forget, says Kevin, that Bob was slowly and methodically poisoning his entire system with the bloody fags, which all his peers had given up decades earlier. 'I think he was nicotine-delusional at times.'

The culture had turned to shit, perhaps.
Ian Wedde visited Sealy Road in the 80s and he and Robin had a long walk on Long Bay Beach, and Robin was gloomy and bitter about the culture in which he was trying to keep something going. Value systems had shifted. He saw no hope. He told Ian local writing, publishing and journalism had all gone to shit, and that he felt *Islands* was no longer esteemed.

The whole country had turned to shit.
It's worth recalling (this is me, Adam, talking now) that in the early 1980s Robert Muldoon was PM, the Springboks toured and the economy was a shambles. There was optimism when Lange's Labour won the '84 election, but then Roger Douglas administered economic chemotherapy and the money-market barbarians and corporate raiders started building their glass towers in the city. What member of the lefty literati wasn't a bit depressed?

His magazine had become irrelevant.
Magazines have a lifespan, says Ian Wedde, and the literary nationalism that had defined *Islands* was being overtaken as academia embraced new ways of working – the 'death of the author' thing, which said readers made texts, not just the writer, and so on. Robin was mistrustful of the academy and 'theory', so as the years passed *Islands* was starting to miss the boat.

Hang on a minute. Perhaps it hadn't.
Not so, says C. K. Stead. Wedde's a terrific poet but he was on the leading edge of all that stuff, so he would say that. Fact is, *Islands* was relevant and publishing the best writing right to the end. Robin was just too slow and he let it drift away, and watching it happen Stead felt 'puzzled and exasperated'.

Things just fall apart.
Maybe, says Bill Manhire, there just comes a time when things stop working the way they used to – you get a bit of arthritis in the head as well as the body.

Bulldozers.
The half-wild idylls of Barnes Road and Sealy Road were stands against the spirit-cramping nature of suburbia. So I do wonder, says Bill, what it meant for Robin and Lois to return to Torbay, out on the northern fringe of Auckland, only to watch the bulldozers and motorways reach out and eat the North Shore.

Envy.
And one might get pretty pissed off, says Bill, if you were an editor living a hand-to-mouth existence and you kept noticing there were other people, third-raters who cared about writing and writers far less that you did, who were on comfortable salaries doing hackwork in academia and publishing.

Pain.
His hips hurt a lot. Maybe, as Rachel said at the funeral, that's why he was cranky. Except the timing's off: he hit peak nastiness in the mid-80s when his hips weren't really so bad, and by the time they got so terrible they needed replacing he'd actually cheered up a bit.

Losing his parents.
A few years before he died, Dad told my sister Ruth he'd really tried to get Lois to understand how profoundly upset he was by his father's death. He'd even broached the subject by asking Lois what the worst thing that had ever happened to her was, and she'd said such-and-such, but to his dismay she hadn't asked him the same question back. He'd wanted to tell her that the worst thing that had ever happened to *him* was the death of his father, but she didn't ask!

When Ruth told me this I felt a flush of familiar teenage anger. This was quintessential Dad – he'd constructed things in such a way that *his* failure to talk about *his* darkest thoughts became *Mum's* fault. Unbelievable.

He was more direct with other confidants though. He told Greg O'Brien, who was then in his 20s and had recently fallen out badly with his own father, to make peace with him as soon as possible, 'because if your Dad died you would take this to your grave as a piece of unresolved business'.

When Dad's mother Winifred died in 1988 he told Jenny Bornholdt he now felt orphaned and terribly depressed, just like he had when Ernest had died. She was impressed at the willingness of a guy of his generation to talk so openly. She asked him if he'd thought about antidepressants.

Feminism.

As I write about Dad's insane reaction to Mum taking a teaching course I start to wonder if I've been underestimating the power of the zeitgeist. Perhaps his treatment of her was less about two individuals and more about a specific, strange moment in the history of sexual politics.

The 1980s was when second-wave feminism became mainstream: you didn't need to read de Beauvoir or Friedan or Steinem, because there were posters everywhere stating Girls Can Do Anything, featuring cartoons of women holding welding torches and hammers. Middle-aged music teachers were realising they were lesbians and banishing the husband to the garden shed so the lover could move in. One of my favourite high-school teachers had a badge she'd sometimes pin to her jacket, which went:

which I greatly admired because it was righteous and politically bold, but also slightly titillating (it doesn't take much if you're a teenage boy).

And yes, Dad was progressive compared to most men of his generation. He published a relatively large number of women, especially in the latter years of *Islands*.* He truly thought women writers were just as good as the guys. He had quite long hair and his son's was even longer for a time. He taught his daughters they could be anything they wanted. He was ahead of the wave.

But then the wave broke over his head, and he turned out to be just one of the guys – part of a cohort of confused middle-aged men all over the western world who were freaking out because their wives, who'd committed themselves to housewifery and docility while living in a different era, had come to realise they didn't have to put up with that sort of shit, especially now the kids had just about left home. Reactions varied, but I'm pretty certain Dad wasn't the only politically enlightened man who responded to a perceived threat of emasculation by turning into some weird, re-masculinised version of himself – a prick, in other words.

---

* His final 1972 *Landfall* had 25% female contributors. *Islands* 1 of the same year had none, but the figure rose thereafter – *Islands 2*, *3*, *4* and *5* had 4%, 4%, 8% and 19% respectively – and plateaued at around a third of contributors: 27% in *Islands* 17 (1977); 38% in *Islands 26* (1979); 29% in *Islands 34* (1984); and 31% in the final edition *Islands 38* (1987). In his correspondence he defended his record. To Sue Vaassen in December 1972 he wrote: 'Why this fiction that I'm an anti-feminist? I love 'em (& try and leave 'em) all, and there's a lot of Ms in ISLANDS 2&3. Fortunate that you can take that abbreviation in two ways.' Then again, he told Riemke Ensing in 1974 that he was 'horrified' at her plan for an anthology of NZ Women Poets, partly because she'd likely end up with 'a collection of work of doubtful quality', and because it would destroy 'any work by women writers to be accepted as, simply, writers'. In 1977 he wrote to *Star* columnist Valerie Davis complaining about her inference that male editors 'consciously or unconsciously have tended to overlook women's writing'. 'I've been publishing work by people (men & women) for a number of years [. . .] I think without fear or favour'.

Zeitgeist excuses nothing. You need have no more sympathy for him on this account than you'd have toward a plantation owner inconvenienced by slavery's abolition. All the same, I think it's something.

18. Return to Damascus

So, BACK HERE. Me and Dad in his office. Kerosene and tobacco in the air, long skinny galley proofs in front of Dad, which he's correcting with his red BIC pen, the kind with the yellow top and little red clicker and a clear plastic barrel where you can see the skinny ink-tube inside, and around us papers, books, manuscripts, magazines stacked high like we're in the archives room in a Terry Gilliam movie.

I'm 15 and I'm gripped by the story we're proofing, the one Dad will shortly publish, about the 1930s great-grandmother who sells biscuits to save up for a fur coat then loses the coat because her mean husband pawns it and keeps the cash, a story about patriarchy and power and control; and part of the reason I'm gripped is it's been only a few weeks since Dad went crazy and sabotaged Mum's attempts to complete a language-teaching course. I can't believe he can't see the irony.

That's how I remember it. It's vivid. It's the anecdote I told a friend a couple of years ago, which he reckoned I could almost build a book on. That's why you've already read it in Chapter 2.

It's not true, though. Since writing the chapter, I've checked dates and read letters, and I've found the story Dad and I were proofreading and read it again. It's by Anne Kennedy – 'Damascus', the lead story in *Islands* 37, which was published in 1986, so I've got the year right. But Mum didn't do her ESOL course till 1988, which means Dad's upending of her study table was years off. If I was even angry with him that day it had to be about something else.

My recollection of the short story itself is mangled too. 'Damascus' is set in the 1890s, not the 1930s. The great-grandmother bakes cupcakes not biscuits, and she saves for years not months. Her husband isn't cruel, just traditional – 'no wife of mine will work' – and he doesn't refuse to buy her a coat; she just realises it's unaffordable and never asks. There's not even a pawn shop – I think I must have borrowed that from Roald Dahl's cheesy adultery-revenge tale 'Mrs Bixby and the Colonel's Coat' from his kinky short-story collection *Kiss Kiss*, one of those books I used to read over and over.

In Anne Kennedy's story, the patriarchal oppression is all internalised – great-grandmother abandons her coat voluntarily after catching sight of her husband in the street and losing her nerve. He never knows there was a coat. It's a far more clever and nuanced tale than the heavy-handed version I reconstructed over a few decades of retelling a small tale about my wicked father.

Worse: in the Turnbull Library, I find a letter from Dad to Anne where he thanked her again for the story and wrote: 'I sat the family down this afternoon (rarely do it these days) and read your story to them [. . .] the story was much enjoyed.'

I can't decide if this improves my own story or ruins it. He liked her story so much he wanted to share it with Mum? And she liked it? And they were getting on well enough that he'd even bother? Is it possible that I actually remember the story because of this cosy family read-through rather than a kerosene-scented proofreading session?

It's unsettling. If I've misremembered this, what else have I got wrong?

Much of what I've written so far is supported by documents: by a photo, a birth certificate, a newspaper cutting, a letter, a diary, an email. Where it's not, I haven't exactly made stuff up, but I've taken a few guesses. I *think* I remember a tantrum-smashed pudding bowl, but maybe it just bounced on the floor and I've Photoshopped in a different memory from a less dramatic crockery incident. In Chapter 16 I had placed Emma the dog's body under a bed of dahlias, until I discovered a letter where Dad said it was a rose she was fertilising and even specified the cultivar (I'd already corrected that sentence before you read it).

I'm worried too that I might have exaggerated my memories; that I'm trying to squeeze *Angela's Ashes* out of a situation that was really more *Cider with Rosie*. It's been reassuring, then, to find some things were actually worse than I remember. I was sure the bullying I got because of my long hair had been trivial by the time I reached high school, but I recently bumped into a schoolmate who reminisced about the time some fuckwit in Third-Form drama class grabbed me by the hair and swung me around his head like a Scottish hammer-thrower. I simply don't remember that.

I had lunch with another school friend, Anton, and told him I was writing a chapter about the 1980s, a time when he was at Sealy Road a lot.

'Are you going to use the butter thing?'

'What butter thing?'

'When I had meals at your place Robin wasn't talking to Lois, so he'd get other people to. You know – "Anton, could you please ask Lois to pass me the butter?"'

No memory of that either.

So I've got some things out of order. I've forgotten things. Some stories may be hybrids – *this* moment at *that* location with *those* people, like those picture books where you flick the pages to make a person with dinosaur feet, belly-dancer body and spaceman head. It's not just me. People I interviewed contradicted each other and themselves, mixed up their years and, just occasionally, may have lied to me.

Yet the constituent parts are still true. The colour of a pen, the smell of a room, the way Dad's face would turn red when he was angry. And you don't forget mood either – the sour stomach of a silent, glowering mealtime, the half-defensive embarrassment of bringing a new friend home, the sober joy of helping your father make books.

After reading the real Anne Kennedy story I consider going back and fixing Chapter 2, but I don't. I leave it there as a caution to myself, or maybe to my reader, to be wary of a striking irony or tidy symmetry. Anyway, the most important line of Anne's story is probably the final one, and I remembered that more or less correctly: 'Greatgrandmother got it all wrong,' says the narrator. 'It's the men who bought the coats.'

You can't nail things down. Dad was a chauvinist pig and a great supporter of women artists. He truly loved Mum and he really hated her. He was awful. He was wonderful.

My entire teens, I'd have you believe, were overshadowed by the depression or existential crisis or whatever it was that visited my father, which was linked to the demise of his publishing career and a crisis in his marriage. And that's the truth, just not the whole truth.

In the Turnbull Library, in one small folder of Dad's 1988–90 correspondence, here is what I found:

– A letter from a poet asking ever so tentatively if Robin would mind terribly if he resubmitted elsewhere the poems Robin has been sitting on for a terribly long time;

– A note from Timaru Public Library, curious about what has happened to the past two years' issues of *Islands*;

– A letter from the Literary Fund requesting an audited financial annual report (I can just hear Dad's sardonic 'Ha!');

– An uncashed cheque for $50 from Janet Frame for her *Islands* subscription, with a note saying keep the change as a donation;

– A letter from Auckland University English lecturer Brian Boyd asking if Robin would think again about allowing the university to support *Islands* on the condition of 'your having absolute editorial control as long as you chose to remain editor'.

All *that* in your mailbox at once. But there's also a poem Jenny Bornholdt wrote after visiting us at Sealy Road around Christmas 1988. Jenny had typed the poem out and sent it to Dad with a note saying it was going to be in her next poetry collection.

Summer

Driving in the green car. Talking. Summer and he feels he might
have bought the shoes before he knew how to tie the laces.
We go to Long Bay with Adam and meet Robin heading up
from the
beach to wash sand from his feet. Dad says Adam Dad but
Robin takes a while to recognise him without his book. He'll go
home, he says, and put the jug on.
Surf chunky and water so warm it is no surprise.
Above us, men with wings hover around the cliffs.
Tea on the verandah with Robin. New shoots from the kiwifruit
vines wave tenderly in the warm air. Babacos dump ripe on the
ground (make the baby wear a helmet in the sandpit). Red snap-
dragons cluster by the step.
Feeding the chickens, Robin picks up a small egg. Listen, he says,
And I hold it to my ear, warm, and hear the small beak tapping.

19. Getting better all the time

For Robin Dudding, possibly the best thing about the 1980s was that eventually they ended.

It was the decade *Islands* died, his father died, his mother died, and his marriage nearly did too.

It was when all his children got fed up with him, establishing grudges that would never entirely fade. Near decade's end we met and co-wrote a letter to him saying we were angry, that we all found his behaviour intolerable, that we were unhappy that he was unhappy, that we didn't like coming home because of him, that it felt like he was cancelling out all the good things of previous years, that we were sick of tiptoeing around and trying to gauge his moods and seeing his back as he walked away, and that we really hated the way he was treating Mum.

I have no memory what his reaction to the letter was. It's quite possible he didn't give us one.

It's also curious, given how clear it seems now that he was suffering from something like depression, that the word doesn't appear in our letter. Perhaps we were being thick, but I think it's more to do with the fact that Prozac didn't reach the market until 1987 and wasn't mainstream till years after that. Depression wasn't taboo exactly, but nor was it on everyone's lips the moment someone became unaccountably grumpy and mean. Urging him to see a shrink wouldn't have crossed our minds – Dad talking about his feelings at a stranger's behest was unimaginable.

If it had even occurred to me to think about Dad in psychiatric terms, whatever it was that ailed him seemed far too energetic – too much shouting and stomping – to be 'depression', which I thought of as that thing where you couldn't get out of bed.

All the same, as the new decade began, things started, very slowly, to get a little better. Freelance work had come and gone, including stints writing a books-world column for the *Listener*, but in late 1990, just before I left home, he got a permanent sub-editing job there, working under chief sub-editor Tom McWilliams and alongside his old crony Kevin Ireland. Tom, Kevin and Bob, three grizzled former editors of *Mate* magazine, reunited four decades later and putting headlines and captions on stories by the likes of Gordon Campbell and Diana Wichtel, Finlay Macdonald and Marion McLeod.

However, for Dad a regular job like this, especially in journalism, was an admission of defeat. He took the sub-editing seriously and found the usual pleasures in working with words, but he was still back in the wretched, cynical, sensationalising trade he'd escaped when he quit the *Auckland Star* in 1959.

A steady, well-paid job was also a capitulation to conformity, and he moaned continually about it – he hated the motorway commute from the Shore and the polluted city air choked his lungs; he was surrounded by sloppy writing and fools; the new editor was a philistine and someone had let accountants into the building.

I'm not being facetious when I say it bothered him to work for the sake of money. While considering whether to apply to be managing editor at Auckland University Press a few years earlier, he'd told a friend the steady income was a 'huge attraction', but this seemed 'of itself, to be cogent reason for not applying: I mean it is hardly the correct motivation for job-vocation'.

Yet he enjoyed the novel experience of solvency, buying himself new running shoes and an expensive racing bike, treating himself to a few beers at the London Bar after work. As Kevin would say to him when they slunk out of the Dominion Road offices for a lunchtime curry and a beer, 'Better than bloody starving in Torbay, eh Bob?'

And when he was playing ping-pong in the *Listener* lunchroom you'd catch glimpses of the mad joy (and vicious competitiveness) that always overcame him when he had a ping-pong paddle in his hand.

At home I noted with narrowed eyes that none of Dad's newfound wealth seemed to make it as far as Mum's pocket. He was as nasty to her as ever; was still short-tempered most of the time. Some of the black cloud followed him to work, where he'd grunt and sigh about the fatuousness of something Joseph Romanos had written in a sports column, or a particularly conceited sentence in a Gordon Campbell interview. He'd roll his eyes and huff if some uptight colleague asked him to obey the new rules banning smoking at his desk. His default expression was thunderous.

The ghost of *Islands* haunted him. He'd tell *Listener* arts and books editor Chris Bourke that he had all the material for the next edition ready to go, if only he could get the funds together.

Yet for all his bitching, I think being forced to interact daily with people on the magazine and in the wider office helped pull him out of his deep funk. He became very fond of some of his workmates, and was seen more often as lovable curmudgeon than unapproachable misanthrope.

There was sometimes a twinkle behind the scowl and he was interested in people. He quietly extracted the life stories of just about everyone in the building, with a level of attention inversely related to their corporate status. He knew the secrets of courier drivers, secretaries and cleaners, yet couldn't bring himself to use the name of the company accountant, instead referring to him as 'the poison dwarf' (and to be fair, the man was very short and quite unpleasant). He talked intently about books and films and music with the writers and other subs, and if someone wanted advice from an old man who'd been around a bit he was happy to give it.

Chris Bourke, especially, was delighted to find yet another literary legend slumming it in the subbery, and was grateful whenever Robin slipped him a suggestion for the ideal book reviewer, and when he introduced him to Dennis McEldowney, the gentle former AUP editor and walking literary encyclopaedia.

Soon after Dad got the job I left home and was flatting in the city, playing in bands and living hand-to-mouth. Dad nepotistically set up some sub-editing shifts for me, and I shared none of his qualms about being motivated by money.

I barely visited home. I presumed he was still being vile to

Mum but at least I wasn't there to see it, and on the days we were in the same office I'd separate Jekyll from Hyde as ever. We'd play ping-pong in the lunchroom, and he'd discreetly coach me so it looked like I knew how to be a sub-editor. I joined him and Kevin for curry and beer, and we observed the usual separation of things we could talk about and things we couldn't.

Soon after that I took a plane to London and didn't come back for three years. My sisters kept me updated about the latest outrages, such as Dad's refusal to attend Mum's graduation, but they also reported that lately, when they were out at Torbay, they'd noticed Dad sometimes talked to Mum in a civil tone of voice. He was, it seemed, becoming a little bit less awful.

The other thing they said was that Dad didn't seem very well. As ever, he was smoking like a train and coughing like he was on the brink of expelling pieces of lung, but he was also in increasing pain from the arthritis in one of his hips, which probably needed replacing.

He tried to stare down his illnesses by doing as much swimming, running, cycling and netball as he could bear. The exercise possibly helped offset the decline of his lungs, but it didn't do much for the hip. His deeply ingrained inability to engage constructively with bureaucrats meant he joined the waiting list for his first hip operation years later than he should have, and in Auckland's social netball circles he was starting to make a name for himself as that mad old bearded guy from the *Listener* who could barely walk, but who'd trundle up and down the court, limping and puffing and farting, and occasionally letting out bloodcurdling yelps of pain.

20. Emails north

He got older. He got sicker. He got nicer, slowly. I used to think the two things were connected – that he'd looked at his failing body and realised no one was going to nurse him in his dotage if he remained alienated from his entire family. Either that or the illness was robbing him of the energy and breath it takes to be a fulltime arsehole.

I'm less sure now. I think if he could have stopped being mean and miserable by sheer force of will he'd have done so years earlier. As it was he remained cantankerous and snappy, still exercised his crazed iron grip over every crumbling square inch of Sealy Road, still knew how to win an argument by saying nothing or limping away – but somehow the bitterness, the *fury* of the 1980s faded away.

Steroid inhalers, antibiotics, anti-inflammatories and painkillers. Drugs to offset the sore guts from the anti-inflammatories, and sedatives because the steroids mucked up his sleep. He left the *Listener* after six years, aged 61, partly because he didn't have the stamina for a full day's work. A couple of years before that, I'd been visiting New Zealand and went in with him to work. As we inched down two long flights of internal staircase, ex-prime minister David Lange was centimetring up the other way, heading for an interview with a *Listener* writer. Lange was slowly dying of a blood disease; Dad had clogging lungs and a hip joint like broken glass, so the two of them shared the staircase for such a long time it started to feel awkward.

He got one new hip at 62 and another at 66. He quit the cigarettes but it was way too late for his smoke-brittled lungs. Emphysema, said the specialist. You're not going to drop dead soon, but when you die this is what it'll be from.

I returned to New Zealand then left again. I married. I lived in Newcastle then London. I didn't feel quite right. I missed Auckland's summers and the hot pools up at Waiwera, but London seemed too full of promise to leave quite yet. I felt flat. One mid-winter night I woke in a panic from a dream that Dad had died and sort of cried for a bit because it felt interesting to have a strong emotion, even if it was borrowed from a dream, but then stopped because it seemed silly.

I wondered how long you survived with emphysema.

Dad asked if I could be with him in New Zealand during his first hip replacement operation, so I came home for a long Torbay summer and we went for faltering walks of gradually increasing length, mostly to the beach. He complained constantly but took pride in ticking off the distance targets on the colour-coded exercise calendar I drew up for him on a piece of A3.

I enjoyed the time warp of being home and sleeping in my old room. I noted with no surprise at all that Dad was a tyrannical invalid, a 'grumpy spider in the middle of the room' as one sister put it, constantly asking people to fetch and carry or do minor DIY repairs to his precise specifications. But I also noticed that, most of the time, he was OK towards Mum. At times he was tender, almost flirty.

I knew I should be pleased but I actually felt squeamish. It seemed wrong, like he must be pretending. Or maybe it bothered me because it meant all that indignation I'd felt on Mum's behalf for half my life had been in vain. She was letting him resume affections, just like that. Part of me, still 15 years old, wanted some sort of conspicuous public apology. Still, it didn't look as if Mum minded being an object of renewed affection. She seemed to have decided to get on with enjoying the good bits of her marriage as they came, and ignoring or forgiving or forgetting the rest.

I bought an old computer before I left and set up an email address for the two of them – woodspring@xtra.co.nz, in honour of the Woodspring Cottage plaque that was still on the side of the garden shed, termite-ravaged and peeling. By the time I got back to cold London, the first emails from Dad bragging of his distances walked and strokes swum were waiting for me.

Mum emailed to say she and Dad had recently been dragged to a family get-together by four of her sisters who'd noticed it was their wedding anniversary. It was a lovely day, said Mum, but 40 years of marriage seemed 'a funny thing to celebrate'.

Dad emailed much more than Mum: updates on the state of chooks and tomatoes and my sisters' families, lists of the books he was reading and the beach swims he'd had that week, fondly gruff complaints about Mum's hopelessness with her newly earned driving licence and her shitty broken-down car (he wouldn't let her drive his). I replied with my own garden statistics, existential angst, boasts about my latest Fleet Street job or continental weekend jaunt, and what I was reading. When *Landfall*'s editor asked Dad to do some book reviews he said no but gave her my contacts instead, then gently edited my reviews before I filed them.

He read a Joe Bennett newspaper column in the *Herald* and thought it was so good that he typed the entire thing into an email to me, I guess because he wasn't able to read it out to me over breakfast in person. He said he'd just been to the big Hotere exhibition at the Auckland gallery and found it 'incredible that the juxtapositions of colours should be so moving'.

I said I'd been to see the new *Planet of the Apes* movie and there'd been one character, an elderly chimpanzee with greying facial hair, who was the spitting image of him, and I enclosed an image to prove it.

Keyboard to keyboard across 18,000km we were as close as I remember us ever being.

In 1999, '20 years and 5 million cigarettes too late' as he put it in an email to Bill Manhire, Robin Dudding finally made it to the northern hemisphere – a shoestring tour with Mum of the UK and the continent, with stopovers each way in Buenos Aires, where he felt exhilarated and instantly at home amid the heat, the stink, the terrible slums, the racial mix, the amazing Italian food.

Inspired by some mad travel guide they'd read, they were fanatical about travelling light, mostly so they would never have to wait for checked-in luggage on arrival at an airport. Given how fast Dad could walk, such haste hardly seemed necessary, but sure enough, when they came into the arrivals hall at Heathrow within minutes of their plane's touchdown, they each carried just a tiny daypack for the three months ahead: more than enough room for passports, a change of undies and Dad's extensive medicine cabinet.

This was midway between hip operations, so he had one goodish leg and one in a manageably early stage of collapse. The real problem was his breathing. The corticosteroids he inhaled bought him several days of tolerable lung function at a time, but they were so toxic to the rest of his body that they had to be rationed. He'd calculate which were the days he really needed to breathe and which days he could busk it, but even a minor cold or the previous day's over-exertion could mess it all up and he'd find himself at the door of his lodgings in Pisa, faced with a 63-step climb to his room on a day when ten steps was Everest.

His illness made some days hellish but he was mostly gleeful. He got hooked on Spain's cheese, olives, red wine and hard bread, was entranced by Venice, Paris, Zurich, Cahors, Bath, London, Madrid and Barcelona, and the people he found there.

'One bonus of being me,' he told Manhire, 'is that I don't rest until I've made people talk to me (in whatever language).'

A few weeks before they arrived, my wife Catriona and I nearly bought a flat in Camden, but as we got closer to making a final offer I felt a sense of rising panic.

I really hadn't wanted to come back to England, yet I did it anyway, and now I didn't like being here. I hadn't wanted to live in Newcastle or get a newspaper job – but I did both anyway. I sort of wanted to go home but didn't seem able to do anything about making it happen. House ownership looked like shackles, the long line of zeros in the price the links of a chain. The voice in my head was screaming *Nooooo!* again, and this time I decided to listen to it.

I said we couldn't buy the flat, then followed my logic to its conclusion. If I was unable to commit to buying a house, maybe that meant I wasn't able to commit to this marriage either. Didn't it? Yes? No? Maybe?

Yes, I decided. It did. Definitely. I was sure.

I informed my wife that we were doomed but – ahem – as she knew, my parents were about to visit and this was the trip to Europe that Dad had been waiting for for half a century and he was sort of dying so he wouldn't get another chance, probably. Would she mind terribly if we delayed telling anyone about the marriage implosion I'd talked myself into? It'd only be a few months and then we could split and everything would be fine.

It's the most appalling favour I've ever asked of anyone. She agreed, presumably for the benefit of my parents rather than me, though I didn't really want to hear too much detail about what she felt about anything at this point.

The situation was ridiculous, barbaric. Sadistic almost. I cringe with shame at the memory. The four of us took jolly day trips around London together. We'd spend a convivial evening with my parents then head off to our room to argue briefly, maybe cry, then rigidly share a bed. We went ahead with a plan to rent an apartment in Tuscany for a week, taking not only my parents but also my Scottish mother-in-law. Brilliant.

I suspect that, just like the time that boy at school swung me around his head by my hair, there are unpleasant moments from the visit to Italy that I've quietly blanked, but as I recall it, this covertly tragic week was almost entirely enjoyable, and we overcame the marriage-on-the-rocks problem mostly by ignoring it.

We were happy idiots. I rented a car at the airport and almost drove us under a speeding oil tanker at the first highway intersection because I was looking the wrong way. A toll-booth attendant lost patience with my total incomprehension and took €75 off me for using 2km of his autostrada (we later calculated we could have driven to France and back for that price). We were kicked off a beach after discovering you had to pay to sit on the sand.

My parents loved the narrow streets, the time-weathered architecture and locals. Catriona's mother, on her first-ever trip to Europe, overcame the language barrier at the village delicatessen by oinking, mooing and clucking at the man behind the counter till she got the ham, milk and eggs she needed. We were hugely entertained when Catriona went to a pharmacy to ask for something for her cystitis and was given an antiseptic drug that you can't get in the UK called Mictasol Bleu, which turns your wee a shocking blue, and I was so intrigued by it that I took one to see if it would turn my wee blue too.

Never a stoic, Dad complained unceasingly about his hips, lungs, guts, bank balance. Yet he was unstoppable, grunting and grumbling his way across a Himalayan range of pensione steps, aircraft boarding stairs and steep Spanish lanes.

'However decayed and broken-down I feel,' he told Bill Manhire, 'I still think I'm OK . . .'

Mostly true, but not always.

Catriona and I rejoined them in Spain for another week of pretending everything was fine, which it was, until all of us bar Mum came down with a vicious flu. For Catriona and me it meant a couple of days in bed aching all over and coughing, but for Dad it meant a frightening contraction of his world.

In Madrid he walked out of a café thinking the rest of us were just behind him. By the time he realised we weren't coming he didn't have enough strength to turn around, reopen the heavy spring-loaded door and fetch us, but nor could he make it back to our nearby hotel alone. When we finally came out a few minutes later he was leaning against a wall gasping, face contorted, skin grey, spitting with anger.

'Where the *fuck* were you?' he hissed between gasps, and though he was hunched over, for a moment he seemed bigger and scarier than he had for years. It was dinnertime in the 1980s all over again, only this time he didn't have the strength to smash a plate, let alone stalk off. We bit our tongues and apologised, then crawled back to the hotel together, where eventually he stopped shaking with rage and took an extra dose of steroids a few days earlier than he'd really wanted to.

After they'd returned to New Zealand and the much-delayed split was finally enacted, I fell silent for weeks until Dad's emails demanding a sign of life got the better of me and I confessed our secret. He replied with a rare telling-off, though mainly to say he felt wounded we'd not trusted them enough to say what was going on, and for making him feel stupid for not spotting anything amiss.

He wrote as many emails to Catriona as to me while we were apart, and a year later, when we'd finally untangled most of the knots I'd tied myself in, and we were warily but definitely back together, he was very happy, and happier still when we said we were having a baby, and that we'd be coming back to New Zealand once that was done.

Four months before our planned return to New Zealand, Dad finally reached the top of the queue for his second hip replacement. But rather than being relieved he was terrified. Somehow he'd developed a theory that the state of his lungs meant he'd probably die under anaesthesia. He was fretful and morbid, unable to sleep.

It seemed unlikely to me – surely the surgeons wouldn't be offering the operation if they expected it to kill him – but over the course of an ambiguous, side-stepping phone call it became obvious that he'd really like me to be there for the operation, so I booked a fortnight's leave and a flight to New Zealand. If all went well I could draw up a post-op exercise chart for him like last time, and if not, well . . .

Anna emailed me the day after the phone call. After I'd told Dad I was coming, he'd slept through the night for the first time in weeks. He was looking the healthiest he'd been in six months. She and Mum had talked about it, and they reckoned he was still haunted by that trip to Hastings to see his father, when he'd arrived five hours too late. Dad couldn't bear the idea of that happening to me too. He was, he'd told Anna, very very pleased I was on my way home.

21. Sixteen things my father taught me

Everything will go wrong.
Cars won't start. Roofs will leak. Tools will be lost and when they're found they will be broken or blunted or out of petrol. Coffee will spill on important papers. Eggshell will fall into the bowl when you're making scrambled eggs. Wasps will build nests in your paper archives. There will not be enough money in the bank to cover the bill. There is never enough time. It will always be impossible to find the thing.

Everyone lets you down.
Printers will print the artwork upside down. Typesetters will insert an extra error after you've returned the last proof. There will always be more things wrong with your car *after* it gets back from the garage, and with your teeth after you get

home from the dentist. If you lend a son-in-law a gardening implement he will always bring it back broken. Someone has always moved the thing.

Everything is negotiable.
Most services, including dentistry and car repairs, can be exchanged for a tray of fresh eggs.

How to treat a chicken with scaly leg mites.
Fill a jam-jar with 50% kerosene and 50% engine oil. Hold the chook's body close to calm it, then take one leg and carefully edge it into the jar and leave it there for a few seconds – it stings, so be ready for a bit of wriggling. Repeat with the other leg, then put the chook down carefully so she doesn't flick kerosene and oil all over the place.

How to make an excellent liquid fertiliser.
Fill a large cloth potato sack with spadefuls of compacted shit and straw scraped from the floor of your fowl-houses. Suspend the sack in a 40-gallon drum of water, cover and leave to steep for a few weeks, by which time all the goodness will now be in the black, pungent liquid.

Don't make loud noises near Buff Pekin bantams.
They have weak hearts and if they get a scare they could drop dead on the spot.

A book must have generous gutters.
You shouldn't have to crack the spine just so you can comfortably read all the words on the page.

Baths should always be scalding hot.
Same with showers, though they should always end with a few shocking seconds of 100% cold water to strengthen your heart.

If you wash dishes in hot enough water you don't need detergent.

Walk away from unpleasant situations.
If you're not physically present when an argument's happening, you can't possibly lose.

Walk away from pleasant situations.
If there are people visiting and everyone's having a nice time, no one will notice if you slip away for half an hour to feed the chooks or take a quick siesta.

Always take a siesta.

Old things are better, even if they're broken.

Money is mostly bad.

It's hard to beat a really good Chinese meal.

Catch the wave just before it breaks.
Any later and it's all foam. Any earlier and it won't pick you up.

22. Summer

On the last Saturday of January 2016 the cicadas are shrieking like tinnitus and it's too hot to eat dinner at home so I fill a chillybin with food and bottles of iced water and we drive to Waiake. It's no longer my nearest beach – not even Mum lives in Torbay now – but it's still only 10 minutes' drive. I'm back on the Shore and in the summer holiday months, when the central city becomes an empty, boring furnace, the Shore is still the best place to live.

At Waiake the tide's so low the kids doing bombs off the raft are only up to their chests when they stand back up, gritty mud and cockles sliming between their toes. Once it was four rusty 40-gallon drums lashed together under an algae-slimed wooden platform, but the latest replacement is a prefabricated plastic thing.

There are half a dozen yachts bobbing in the bay, some of them the same ones Dad used to swim past, counting to save his life ('900 backstrokes at dawn, this season's record' he emailed me a few months after his first hip operation), while Mum breast-stroked about the shallows – or, as autumn edged into winter and it got too cold for fair-weather swimmers, while Mum promenaded on the shore telling another walker that in fact she knew that person way out by the boats waving his arms in the air as if in distress; actually he's doing backstroke.

We spread a blanket and some towels near the pōhutukawa that crouches on a low seawall at the north end of the beach. For decades the tree shaded a stretch of shore carpeted with kikuyu, and we'd claim the scratchy-grassed hollow for the day, a shifting cohort of parents, sisters, sisters' boyfriends, school friends and neighbours, there for a quick dip, a day's indolence or something in between. Violent storms in the early 2000s tore the kikuyu away and now it's just sand again.

We spray ankles against sandflies, unpack food, throw a ball for the dog, try to identify our children's heads in the swarm around the raft. They don't seem to have drowned yet.

Waiake increasingly became Dad's gym, especially when one hip or the other made walking impossible. He and Mum befriended other beach regulars, but didn't get all their names. One woman was just The Wife of the Man Who Hides from His Dog. Mr Las Vegas didn't swim, but he walked to keep his weight down and had an overseas trip most years. Flipper Bob once turned up at Sealy Road with five bags of seaweed, and dug Robin's veggie garden over, and The Other Bob gave my nieces his old P-Class yacht after Mum told him they were learning to sail.

In the weeks before his second hip op, Dad was so crippled

he needed a cane all the way to the water's edge, where he'd leave it standing in the sand. After his swim Mum would take it to him to save him limping out of the shallows, until one morning The Other Bob turned up with an attachment he'd fashioned so that Dad could take his stick all the way into the sea and leave it floating, anchored by lead weights in a mesh bag, as he swam.

I walk the length of the beach, taking photos, trying to remember what's changed compared with my earliest memories of Waiake: a missing set of swings, a bus shelter that wasn't there before, a new playground, missing kikuyu, a pōhutukawa that used to be much smaller.

It's such a low tide. The muddy creek at the north end dribbles into a temporary lagoon that stretches across the beach, attracting toddlers to its urine-temperature shallows.

It's so low that the rocks are dry between the headland and the Tor – the clay-yellow nubbin of land that must have disconnected from the main cliff centuries ago. In the summer holiday between intermediate and high schools, Desleigh Jameson and I scrambled to the top with unstated yet clear intent but didn't quite summon the courage to kiss, though I allowed my friends to infer the worst.

I walk into the water and it's so warm there's no surprise. It's too calm for body surfing but that's usually the case at Waiake. It was at Long Bay, our other beach, that Dad showed me how you timed the flat dive shoreward so your momentum combined with the wave's and you got a decent ride so far in that you risked grinding your face into the sand. All summer I've been trying to teach my own kids with a combination of demonstration and impatient yelling, but they always get bored and duck-dive away as I'm trying to explain the physics of why waves break.

By the turn of the millennium, Editor Dudding was long out of the literary game. *Islands* had been officially dead for a decade and he hadn't written a *Listener* headline in years. Mostly he slowly gardened and swam and sat in the sun, with sidelines in limping, coughing and complaining.

He read a lot – out loud if it was a shareable passage and someone was near enough to hear. He sent a swooning email to Catriona after having taken her advice to read A. S. Byatt's *Possession* – it was 'like having a real adventure'. He asked Bill Manhire to explain, seeing he was the clever academic, just what it was that made Colm Tóibín's books so mouth-wateringly addictive. He would read each new Philip Roth as soon as it had arrived at the Browns Bay library.

Mostly, though, he read crime fiction, especially stuff with a comic edge – the semi-fictional adventures of Jewish country-singer-turned-P. I. Kinky Friedman, the witty brutality of Elmore Leonard, the Florida capers of Carl Hiaasen. He also reread a lot of P. G. Wodehouse.

A bibliophile in his dotage can read whatever the hell he likes and arguably you'll find more pleasure, wisdom and craft in a single page of Wodehouse or Friedman than in ten chapters of some well-regarded literary novels. But I always wondered if there was a whiff of sour grapes in his choice of material, a private fuck-you to the world of serious literature, especially New Zealand literature, the tantalising, infuriating thing that had driven him half-mad, all-but-scuttled his marriage and kept him near the breadline all his life.

Or if not sour grapes, perhaps self-preservation: if Kevin

Ireland was right and decades of immersion in gloomy, Polish-style NZ Lit had helped push him into depression, why risk it all again when he could be giggling in his armchair with Bertie Wooster, or picking up the phone with a greeting borrowed from Kinky Friedman: 'Start talking!'

Yet when the literary past called, he didn't snub it. He was quietly chuffed to get an entry in the 1998 *Oxford Companion to New Zealand Literature*, and again when in 2000 Bill Manhire dedicated *Doubtful Sounds*, a collection of Manhire's essays and interviews, to him. A few years after that Bill, once Dad's protégé but now the softly spoken *capo dei capi* of NZ Lit, made him an offer he wasn't allowed to refuse: be guest editor of the 2003 edition of *Best New Zealand Poems*, an online series run by Bill's International Institute of Modern Letters at Victoria University.

The email in which Dad explained to Bill why he should ask someone else instead of him was full of the same half-ironic self-flagellation, agonising doubt and unmistakeable excitement that ran through the correspondence of his *Mate*, *Landfall* and *Islands* days. He listed the reasons for his 'crippling trepidation' about taking the job, which included an inability to understand or judge poetry, his arthritis, an imaginary stomach ulcer, being very busy with a grandson's fundraising sausage sizzle, his disconnection from the literary scene of late and his preference in any case for growing tomatoes, leeks and chickens, and, perhaps most insightfully, because: 'one would like to be famous, notable, useful, contributing . . . but it also seems that temperamentally, I'm a bit unemployable cos I worry myself into a blue funk.'

And yet, he conceded, for all his ignorance of current poetry 'my ears prick up when I stumble across something

I like and it wouldn't do me any harm to stop reading US crime books . . .'

'Hi Robin,' Bill replied. 'I take it that's a yes!'

So over the course of 2003 Dad read most of the New Zealand poetry published in print or online that year, exchanged emails with Bill in which he fretted about how awful some of it was, and early the next year pared it down to the 25 he liked best. For all the protestations he was patently thrilled to be flexing his creaky editorial muscles, and it turned out he recognised most of the poets' names even after his 10 years in the wilderness: here were Jenny Bornholdt and Richard von Sturmer, Bob Orr and Gregory O'Brien, Chris Price and Elizabeth Smither, Peter Bland and Kevin Ireland.

His introductory essay included a warm (if typically backhanded) acknowledgement of Mum's involvement – 'my wife Lois has to accept at least 50 percent of the blame or praise for the present selection; I couldn't have managed without her expert reading'. One of his (her?) selections is a poem by Anne Kennedy, author of the short story 'Damascus', entitled 'I was a feminist in the eighties', something that tickles me rather, though perhaps I'm looking too hard for patterns and echoes.

In the closing paragraphs of his introduction Dad identifies his own patterns and echoes:

> It has been rewarding to greet some old friends in the poetry world – Kevin Ireland, Peter Bland and, particularly, Gordon Challis, whose poem comes from his second collection, published last year, 40 years after his first. So, a personal note here. The first magazine I edited (with one other, David Walsh) was the second issue of *Mate*, in 1958. The contributors to that issue included Gordon Challis,

> Kevin Ireland and Lois Miller (aka Lois Dudding). In several ways, then, *Best New Zealand Poems* 2003 is the last link in a rather slow-growing circle. (As a matter of interest – and some pride – the other contributors to that issue of *Mate* were: Odo Strewe, Peter Fairbrother, Maurice Gee, Alan Roddick, Barry Crump [first publication], Frank Sargeson, John Graham, Charles Doyle and Anthony Stones.)
>
> I believe that magazine gave some pleasure to quite a few people. I hope the same can be said for *Best New Zealand Poems* 2003.

It's an unfamiliar sound, one that hasn't been heard for decades, but this is Robin Dudding blowing his own trumpet. It's something else too, with its talk of a *last link* and a *slow-growing circle.* He's not dead yet, won't be for another four years, but this is the editor's swansong.

In the middle of that year, Catriona gave birth at home to our second child, a girl. Eliza arrived just after 10pm and Mum and Dad turned up soon after to admire their 15th and final grandchild. Six weeks after that, Mum's brain blew up.

It was just after midnight. She'd been in the garden picking snails from her flower garden and flinging them over the fence to the neighbours, rather than kill them. She was going to bed when she suddenly felt weak and lost consciousness.

The night was like a practice run for the night of Dad's death: the same family phone-tree in the middle of the night, the same tearful streetlamp-lit drive from home to the hospital in Takapuna, the same stomach lurch and mental exploration of the possibilities: how do I feel, just hypothetically, if my parent is already dead, or is going to die, or ends up a vegetable? And which would be worse?

At the hospital Mum was behind a curtain on a gurney with an IV drip and an ID wristlet, unconscious through most of it. There were tests and scans, but not much sense of urgency. Treatment appeared to consist mainly of waiting for her to live or to die. As the sky lightened, a doctor showed us the huge ink blot on one side of the CAT scan of Mum's brain, where the blood from a broken vessel was flooding the cranium and putting huge pressure on the brain tissue, rearranging the soft structures like an egg being whisked. The pressure may still be building, said the doctor, and in the worst cases the pressure gets so great the brain starts to squeeze out the hole at the base of the . . .

'Stop!' said one of my sisters. 'We get the picture.'

Mum's brain chose to remain inside her skull, but when she woke the next day she couldn't walk or talk and her right hand was already starting to curl into itself, like she was holding a handful of grain for scattering to the chooks.

She spent the next four months in a hospital rehab unit, progressing from bed to chair to walker to stick. There was physio for her dead right leg and arm, vocab lists for her mangled speech. Another woman in her ward couldn't speak either, though the pair of them still chatted, yabbering away without words, just *hmmn-hmm-homm-hmm* back and forth between the beds. Nothing, not even the absence of words, was going to stop Mum talking.

Some words returned within days, but they were slippery, untrustworthy things. One afternoon I dropped in just after an earlier visitor had left.

'Who was it?' I asked.

Mum couldn't remember the name. After much stammering, she finally located the part of her brain where she had once stored names of sisters and other important people, and returned with a word.

'Omelette,' she told me confidently. 'Omelette.'

I later figured out it had been her younger sister Corinne.

Eventually she returned home to a house full of new handrails, to be nursed by the husband with failing lungs who, with every passing year, had been depending on her more and more to be his nurse, to fetch and carry and cook, and to feed the chooks because he couldn't make it back up the hill from the fowl-run.

Shortly before she arrived, a contingent of volunteers led by the Waiake Beach regulars, average age 70ish, arrived at Sealy Road with spades and a concrete mixer, and laid a wheelchair-friendly concrete path from front gate to front door.

Recently I wrote a newspaper article about a choir Mum has joined for people with Parkinson's, strokes and other neurological problems. The article opened with my account of her flinging the snails over the fence and heading to bed, but I left out one detail, which is that at the moment her stroke actually struck she and Dad were having sex. A national newspaper somehow felt too indiscreet a place to mention this impressive, appalling detail.

Once home, Mum was Dad's new project, another baby from through the hedge who needed soothing and fattening up.

Shocked by her brush with death and conscious of the likely nearness of his own, Dad became soppier than ever. 'She's the most intelligent woman I've ever known,' he said. He watched admiringly as she struggled to get a trouser-leg over her orthotic ankle-brace. 'Look at those legs!'

After a few weeks, though, he became overwhelmed by the sheer enormity of the task and fell into a proper can't-get-out-bed depression. His GP gave him some pills, and a few weeks later he got up again. A breathing specialist gave him lessons in managing the panic caused by his perpetual breathlessness, and how to make better use of reduced lung function. He and Mum moved in with Ruth for a few weeks. He told Ruth that perhaps clinical depression was what had been wrong with him back in the 1980s, and it was a shame he hadn't been offered happy pills like these back then. Ruth said, 'No shit, Sherlock', or words to that effect.

They returned once more to Sealy Road with its leaky roof and outdoor loo. They muddled along. From time to time my sisters and I would conclude They Really Can't Go On Like This and repair something without Dad's permission, or offer solutions involving a granny flat or a cottage at the bottom of someone's garden, or even, heaven forfend, a retirement village. Tenacity and bloody-mindedness, and a desire by both of them to keep sitting on the porch and looking out over the small forest of rimu and kōwhai and tōtara Dad had planted over four decades kept them there. When he finally got rid of the chooks, it was 'temporary'.

He emailed us great lists of chores: there were plums to pick, tomatoes to stake, feijoas rotting on the ground if someone didn't hurry over, the computer mouse was sticking, could you come and fit the oxygen cylinder so I can keep using it while driving, and I need a lift to the hospital on Wednesday.

Being feeble doesn't mean you can't still be a control freak. His invitation to a weekend working bee contained dozens of demands, including bagging up the chicken shit from the disused fowl-houses and separating out rusty chicken-wire from the 'sound stuff' he would then sell. (How!? To whom!?) The overgrowth around the creek needed cutting and some junk from the front garden could go, but only 'with my guidance'.

In the event, he moved so slowly that he couldn't keep an eye on both front and back gardens at the same time, and I recklessly threw away some pieces of rotten wood without asking him.

Mum slowly got better. Dad slowly got worse. It became impossible to tell who was nurse, who was invalid. He read books to her, brought her food, goaded her into ever-longer walks with her stick. She tip-tap-shuffled about the house, figured out how to make a cup of tea and burn beans on the stove one-handed, and it wasn't long before she could walk further than him, if not faster.

He could still drive, though, and 20 months after Mum's stroke, shortly before high tide on a high-summer Saturday, they drove to Waiake Beach for a new kind of adventure.

Dad was quietly hopeful there'd be someone there they knew and sure enough, as he parked on the yellow lines next to the boat ramp, their old friend Dave Tate was just coming out of the sea.

Dave carried Mum's chair down to the waterline and offered to carry her too, but she turned him down. Instead she inched her way through the soft sand with Dave sweeping the path in front of her, like Raleigh and Queen Elizabeth. She sat in the chair for 20 minutes as the last of the incoming tide wet her ankles for the first time since her stroke. A beach-walker said something funny about mermaids, and a passing physiotherapist who worked with stroke victims introduced herself to say she was impressed by Mum's sea-walk.

Once Mum was safely ashore Dad went for his own swim – not all the way out to the boats seeing it was high tide, but still 450 strokes on his back, his longest swim of the summer yet. Then they drove to Browns Bay in their togs for a café breakfast, and once home Dad fired off a euphoric email to his children about their incredible morning and his joy at bringing home 'one well-fed, happy woman. Love to you all, R'.

There's a photo Anna took of the two of them at Waiake about a year after that. They're sitting in folding chairs on the sand near the boat ramp, shaded by a beach umbrella from the blinding midday sun. Mum is looking at the camera with a half-smile. Dad is looking at Mum.

He's wearing black speedos and a wristwatch. His beard is white and so is most of the rug of spiralling hair on his chest. He's squinting a bit but mostly he looks happy. He's in the sun. He's near-naked. He's got sand under his feet and he can see the sea. He's with her.

Look at it and you know what's coming: 12 final months during which we all discover that whenever you think life with emphysema can't get any worse it actually can. His haggard face at the 50th wedding anniversary meal where he's too breathless to eat. The new bed from the children, the thank-you email, the barked shin, the day in Accident and Emergency. The heart attack and the skittering heartbeat in a hospital bed and the final rattle. The honorary doctorate ceremony he missed. The funeral, the speeches.

So I'll stop here, leave him sitting under the umbrella, soaking up the summer heat on a beach on the North Shore. Because that's the other slow-growing circle: the story of my old man and the sea.

There was once a boy who grew up in the middle of the North Island in the middle of the 20th century, who one teenage summer came north for his military service and discovered an isthmus city of coves and peninsulas, of subtropical heat and humidity, of people who saw the world a little differently.

A few years later he came back and married and bought a house, not far from the water, which he filled with children and cats and dogs and chooks and books. He moved to the South Island for a time, but the place and its people were cold and flat, and he gladly loaded up a van for the drive back to the warm, hilly north, stopping for swims all the way, including one on a beach so carpeted with krill that he had to carry his crying young son across a crunching red desert to the sea.

He swam, and taught his children how to catch a wave with or without a board. He barbecued pipis in beer and butter and set fire to his son's feet with meths. He drove to the beach in a baby-blue Transit van filled with rust and on the way home he stopped for fish and chips. He walked the beaches and cliffs talking about D.H. Lawrence and postcolonial fiction and his troubles. Once, a poet he'd published in one of his magazines wrote a lovely poem called 'Summer', about seeing him at the beach.

He worried too much. He smoked like a back-garden bonfire and made himself ill, yet even as he ran out of puff the seawater kept him afloat longer than anyone expected. He windmilled between boats, counting strokes – not waving, and not drowning. And when he wasn't swimming he could sit next to the forgiving woman whose poem he'd published in his first-ever magazine, and look out at the waves, a white-haired Neptune surveying his domain, Canute in Speedos refusing to give up the fight. In this humid town, as he'd told a friend half a lifetime ago, he still sometimes felt moments of quite intense happiness based on warmth, and beach and hills and green.

Spend a couple of years unearthing your dead father and he starts haunting you. I try to leave him at Waiake Beach but he follows me around.

I've looked at so many photos I can shut my eyes and see him: the quizzical two-fingered scratch of the back of his cocked head when listening carefully, the deliberate eyelash flutter which means he's pulling your leg but isn't going to give you the pleasure of hearing him admit it, the crooked simper for attractive waitresses, the satirically furrowed brow if he's noticed the camera, the authentic scowl if he hasn't.

I'll spot a clever newspaper headline or have a proud parental moment, or finish a new Ian McEwan novel, and the thought flickers then dies: *Dad will like that – must tell him about it . . .*

He's been talking to me from within his letters and emails, but I find it difficult to summon the actual sound of his voice, apart from a general memory of a low, warm timbre and an accent that was definitely, but not strongly, Kiwi.

I have one short recording from a couple of months before he died, salvaged from our answerphone. He had rung to say happy sixth birthday to Noah and missed us, so he just said hi and asked us to call back. His voice was thin and scratchy and he paused every few words for a little more air, but he sounded cheerful, stretching out Noah's name in a sort of ironic sing-song.

By then he hadn't the strength to pick either of our children up, but he'd still read to them whenever he was around, and he had a talent for making Noah laugh. He'd make a huge performance of putting together his nebuliser, like a busker unpacking his juggling pins, before puffing a mist of steroids into the big plastic tube and puffing on it with crossed eyes as Noah giggled till he could barely stand.

In the hot sticky weeks after our picnic at Waiake, I take the kids swimming most evenings at our nearest beach, Mairangi Bay.

It's not a great picnic beach but after a summer cyclone the waves get pretty good. I've abandoned my wave-catching lectures, but one evening I realise Noah is getting the hang of it anyway. He's arching his arms right back and putting his head right down. He's almost timing the dive right – late enough that the wave had shown its power but not so late it's already broken.

A large, smoothly curving wave approaches but he dives too early, realises it's no good and quickly curls up in the water to abort the attempt.

The wave just behind is even better. I'm about to catch it myself when I decide to stop and watch. He waits, looks, turns, dives, and disappears under the foam, but five metres later he's still moving with the wave. He curls to end the ride then stands and turns, pushing water and hair off his face. He looks back at me in triumph, and he's laughing.

Tailfeather

Thanks first of all to the Victoria University Press team – Fergus Barrowman, Ashleigh Young, Kirsten McDougall, Craig Gamble, Kyleigh Hodgson and Holly Hunter – for their warm support and advice from start to finish. Thanks especially to Fergus for agreeing to publish this book in the first place, and to Ashleigh for her punctilious attention to every shonky sentence, missing macron and contestable parenthesis once I'd finally delivered a draft.

I'm grateful to Creative New Zealand for a generous arts grant that made it possible to take time off work to research and write, and to my employers at Fairfax Media, and especially the *Sunday Star-Times*, for their support. A grant from Copyright Licensing New Zealand enabled my research at the Alexander Turnbull Library, where my hand was held by the estimable Jocelyn Chalmers and others. Thanks also to archivist David Murray at the Hocken Library for digging through the collections of Charles Brasch and others.

Much of the book couldn't have been written at all if it weren't for the people who gave their time to talk about my father, and were such good company it never felt like work. Thanks to Rose Beauchamp, Mike Beveridge, Jenny Bornholdt, Chris Bourke, Carol and Mick Delaney, Ian and Gail Dudding, Patrick Evans, Ian Fraser, Wendy Galvin, Maurice Gee, Witi Ihimaera, Kevin Ireland, Kate, Fiona Kidman, Bill Manhire, Tom McWilliams, Beth Nannestad, Gregory O'Brien, Anne Peart, C. K. Stead, Tony Stones and Ian Wedde.

For places to write, encouragement, advice, random facts, assorted favours and early feedback, thanks to Bill and Euphymya Lavelle, Daisy McGlashan and Nicki Pettigrew, Brendan O'Brien, Peter Simpson, Jenny Hellen, Alex Sinclair, Jon O'Malley, *Metro* magazine, and Max and Lucy. Thanks also to Steve Kilgallon, mostly because he wanted to be on the Acknowledgements page, but also because it was a conversation with him that helped get this started.

An early version of Chapter 1 was published in *Landfall* 229, some chunks of Chapter 22 were purloined from a feature written for the *Sunday Star-Times* magazine, *Sunday*, and fragments of Chapter 8 were first written during a workshop run by Deborah Shepard at the Michael King Writers' Centre. Thanks to all concerned.

For kind permission to quote from unpublished correspondence, thanks to James Norcliffe, Maurice Gee, Jack Lasenby, James K. Baxter Trust trustee John Baxter, Janet Frame's literary executor Pamela Gordon, and Martin Crump, son of the late Barry. Harry Watson kindly gave me permission to quote from his mother Jean's novel *Stand in the Rain*. Thanks to Jenny Bornholdt (again) for permission to reproduce her poem 'Summer'. Thanks and apologies to Anne Kennedy for my misremembering of her story

'Damascus'. Glenn Jowitt's mad portrait of my father's head amid a bookshelf of *Islands* appears with permission of the Glenn Jowitt Trust. Paul Buckley's magnificent photo of a Sealy Road backyard ping-pong game is reproduced with Paul's permission.

Much love and many thanks must go, of course, to my family. My mother Lois let me rummage through her letters and photos and life, tolerated all my interrogations, and didn't veto a word when I showed her the draft. She's an amazing woman. My sisters Rachel, Ruth, Melissa, Natasha and Anna have enthusiastically joined me in digging through family photos and memories, and between us we unearthed all sorts of surprises.

The entire exercise, though, would have been impossible without the endless support, encouragement and sharp-eyed first reads of the wonderful Catriona Ferguson. I'm hugely grateful to her and to our children Eliza and Noah, for being so tolerant over the many months when I kept slipping away to read boxes of musty letters and read proofs instead of being a good husband and father. Thanks guys. As for my own father? The things I have to thank him for would fill a book.

Note on font

The font used in this book is Adobe Garamond Pro. The Garamond font family is based upon the typefaces created by the famed French printer Claude Garamond in the 16th century. This serif face was created by Robert Slimbach and released by Adobe in 1989; its italics are influenced by the designs of Garamond's assistant, Robert Granjon.